ANTHONY BASHFORD

Emergency Services Humorous History Book

.

This book is dedicated to all the men and women of
"The Big Seven"

Corrections Officers, Dispatchers, EMS Personnel, Firefighters, Law
Enforcement Personnel, Military Personnel, and Nurses

Without all of you, the world would be chaos.

Contents

V   Medical Mavericks

VI   The Caring Chronicles

VII   Military Marvels

I

Dialing Up Danger

Dive headfirst into the heart-pounding world of emergency services in 'Dialing Up Danger.' We'll take you on a roller coaster ride through the birth of 911, the dramatic power of GIS in dispatch, and the occasional intrusion of technology when you least expect it. Imagine binge-watching your favorite T.V. show, only to be interrupted by a stern voice warning you of impending doom. Sounds like a plot twist in itself, doesn't it?

The Birth of 911

The dramatic birth of 911, a tale that rivals the most gripping episodes of your favorite crime show. An adventure back to a time when rotary phones and Morse code were still a thing. The mid-20th century, when emergency calls were as efficient as sending smoke signals across the Grand Canyon.

It all began in the quaint city of Haleyville, Alabama, back in 1968. This wasn't the age of smartphones and instant messaging but the era of dialing numbers on clunky landline phones. You might think that when people found themselves in dire straits, they could simply dial 911 and summon help. But oh, no! It wasn't that straightforward. Back then, you'd dial separate numbers for police, fire, and ambulance, which is about as convenient as juggling flaming torches while riding a unicycle.

These visionaries faced many challenges when trying to sell the 911 dream. Imagine convincing folks that this three-digit number would be their beacon of hope in emergencies. You might as well be peddling magical unicorn rides. Skeptics were everywhere, questioning if this "911" would stick or if it'd go the way of other failed fads like pet rocks and disco.

But lo and behold, Haleyville pulled it off! On February 16, 1968, Rankin Fite picked up that very phone and dialed 911 for the first time, like a modern-day Alexander Graham Bell. And guess what? The phone didn't explode; the earth didn't shake; it was a success! Other cities

3

started to catch wind of this miraculous three-digit code that could summon help with the efficiency of a superhero's distress signal.

Of course, rolling out 911 across the entire nation wasn't a breeze. Convincing all the states, cities, and townships to agree on a standard emergency number was no walk in the park. It's more like herding cats in a bathtub. However, the idea spread like wildfire step by step, eventually leading to the Federal Communications Commission (FCC) declaring 911 as the official emergency number for the entire United States in 1973. They even proclaimed it with their best "Let it be known!" voice.

This revolution in emergency communication was more than just a numerical change. It transformed the way society thought about emergencies. Suddenly, instead of remembering three separate numbers, folks could call one universal number, even if their mind was racing like a squirrel on caffeine.

Ultimately, the birth of 911 is a testament to human ingenuity and the power of persistence. It's similar to persuading the world that sliced bread was indeed the greatest invention since...well, bread. From that humble start in Haleyville, 911 blossomed into a global phenomenon. It's now as ingrained in our lives as emojis in text messages, ensuring that help is just three digits away when needed. So, raise a metaphorical toast to the pioneers who turned an audacious idea into a lifeline, forever changing how emergencies are handled.

In the annals of emergency response, 911 emerged as a lifeline to hope, connecting communities with help in their darkest hours.

The First Emergency Call

That first call on February 16, 1968, would forever change how people reached out for help. Now, if you think this was a casual affair involving a rotary phone and some button-pushing, you're in for a shock.

Rankin Fite, the illustrious Speaker of the Alabama House of Representatives, decides it's high time to test that newfound 911 system. Haleyville, Alabama, was about to become the stage for a telephone revolution, not the "call from your mom" kind. Fite picked up the receiver and dialed those iconic three digits in a move that would make even the boldest texter envious. Oh, the anticipation! Would it work? Would it connect? Would the universe collapse in on itself?

And just like that, a voice crackled on the other end – none other than Tom Bevill, a U.S. Representative. Now, I don't know about you, but that must have been a pretty important call, right? Or perhaps Bevill was just waiting by the phone, hoping someone.., anyone, would call.

The conversation that followed was likely a masterpiece of small talk. "Hey, Tom, it's Rankin. Just checking if this 911 thingamajig works." And Tom, being a communication specialist, probably responded with something like, "Well, Rankin, it seems to be working. Now, if you'll excuse me, I have to get back to pretending to do important things." Thus, the first 911 call became a historical tale of testing the waters and ensuring the operator didn't take a nap.

But here's the kicker – this wasn't the first "real" emergency to grace the 911 system. Nope, that distinction is shrouded in mystery, like a vintage phone booth in a foggy alley. Records are about as scarce as patience in rush hour traffic, and historians are left scratching their heads, wondering who had the honor of making that memorable call.

The exciting and slightly anti-climactic beginning of the 911 emergency dispatch system. Rankin Fite and Tom Bevill forever etched in history as the pioneers of dialing for help. From a mundane test call in the sleepy town of Haleyville to the global lifeline it is today, 911 has come a long way. So next time you dial those digits, remember the days when it all began in Haleyville, Alabama.

With a simple call for help, the first emergency call marked the beginning of a lifeline that would save countless lives.

VoIP and Next-Gen 911

I n the not-so-distant past, landlines reigned supreme. Picture this: an emergency strikes, you grab the chunky, corded phone hanging on your kitchen wall (because that's where phones lived back then), and you dial 911. The call connects to a dispatcher who, if you're lucky, can trace your exact location using the magic of landline technology. It was like calling a wizard, albeit a technologically limited one.

But then, like a plot twist in a sci-fi movie, Voice over Internet Protocol (VoIP) stepped into the scene. It was the late '90s, and VoIP made its debut, allowing voice calls to travel through the vast realm of the internet. No more clunky landlines or wizards; now, your voice could traverse the digital highway to reach the ears of a dispatcher.

VoIP was like that excellent new character in your favorite T.V. show - charming and full of potential. And as the years rolled on, it became a blockbuster hit in the world of communication. People ditched landlines in favor of smartphones and computers, and VoIP was their ticket to connectivity.

But here's where the plot thickens. VoIP had a quirk that baffled our trusty emergency services. Traditional 911 calls were easy to trace because landlines were tied to physical addresses. But with VoIP, you could call from just about anywhere with an internet connection. Your options were limitless: a coffee shop, a park, a mountaintop.

This presented a dilemma. How do you send someone help when you're unsure where they are? Enter the hero of our story, Next-Gen 911. This technological upgrade was like the Avengers of emergency services. It could handle more than just voice calls. Think of this: you're in a situation where speaking is risky, so you text 911. Yes, text to 911. Next-Gen 911 introduced this feature, ensuring your plea for help could be silent but still heard.

And it doesn't stop there. Next-Gen 911 is the James Bond of emergency communication. It brought multimedia messaging to the party. Now, you can send pictures and videos to 911. Now, emergency responders have eyes on the scene before they even arrive. It's not just a call for help; it's a live-action thriller in real time.

Location accuracy became Next-Gen 911's pièce de résistance. It demanded that VoIP providers step up their game and provide precise location data. No more vague guesses about where someone might be; Next-Gen 911 can pinpoint your location down to a few meters.

In a technological revolution in emergency communication, VoIP and Next-Gen 911 have teamed up to provide us with an arsenal of tools – from silent texts to real-time images and spot-on locations. A blockbuster movie where the heroes keep getting better gadgets with each sequel.

In this modern era, when a crisis strikes, you can count on more than just the voice on the other end of the line. You can send a cry for help in text, a snapshot of the situation, and an exact location, all thanks to the evolution of emergency communication. It's a thriller that keeps us safe, and it's still being written with each new technological advancement.

In the digital age, VoIP and Next-Gen 911 technology weave a tapestry of connectivity, bringing emergency services into the future.

The Power of GIS in Dispatch

When every second counts, there lies a silent hero: Geographic Information Systems, or GIS. The unsung savior has transformed dispatch centers from mere map-wielding operations into hubs of precision and efficiency.

Our story began in the late 1960s when maps were scribbled on paper, and dispatchers played a real-life Easter egg hunt when trying to locate callers in need. But fear not, for in 1969, the birth of GIS marked the dawn of a new era. The advent of computerized mapping systems allowed dispatchers to bid farewell to their trusty paper maps and say hello to digital mapping. No more frantic flipping through atlases; now, they could pinpoint locations with just a few clicks.

Fast forward to the 1990s, when GIS technology made its grand entrance into dispatch centers. This was when dispatchers realized they could do more than just find addresses; they could track the precise location of callers right down to the square inch. GPS technology danced into the scene, making it possible to trace a call's origin with astonishing accuracy. Dispatchers went from asking, "Can you describe your surroundings?" to confidently saying, "We know exactly where you are."

As the new millennium dawned, GIS technology evolved, becoming the linchpin of dispatch operations. Integrating real-time data from various sources, transforming dispatch centers into veritable control centers.

Dispatchers became orchestrators, directing resources accurately to where they were needed most.

In 2009, a game-changing event occurred – the Federal Communications Commission (FCC) mandated wireless carriers to provide Enhanced 911 (E911) Phase II, requiring them to deliver accurate location data to dispatch centers. No more excuses, no more vague descriptions. GIS technology became the law, and dispatchers were armed with the tools they needed to save lives swiftly.

Today, GIS technology is the magician behind the curtain where resource allocation has become a well-choreographed dance, and response times have been whittled down to mere minutes.

In the world of dispatch, GIS technology is the compass that guides responders to those in need, making every second count.

Wireless 911 and Phase II Location

L ike any good story, technology evolved, and the era of wireless 911 came with it. It's the late 1990s, and mobile phones are making their grand entrance into our lives. No longer tethered to a wall, we could make calls from anywhere. However, this newfound mobility came with a hitch – pinpointing caller locations became a bit like searching for a needle in a haystack.

When wireless 911 started, if you called for help, the dispatcher might as well have asked you to describe the clouds outside because that's how vague location information could be. Similar to shouting into the void and hoping someone would find you.

As technology marched forward, dispatch centers faced a daunting challenge – how to adapt to this increasingly mobile world. That's where Phase II location tracking came in, a game-changer introduced around 2001. Think of it as a GPS system for 911 calls.

Phase II gave dispatchers a superpower. When you made that emergency call, it connected you to a dispatcher and sent your phone's coordinates. Every mobile phone becomes a homing beacon, guiding first responders to your exact spot.

But as with any technological leap, there were some hiccups along the way. Not all wireless carriers were on board immediately, and not all phones were Phase II compatible. So, in some cases, you might still find yourself playing a modern version of hide-and-seek with first responders.

Nonetheless, the introduction of Phase II was a milestone in wireless 911. It transformed those vague "I think I'm near a coffee shop" calls into precise coordinates that could mean the difference between life and death.

In the ever-changing landscape of technology, wireless 911 and Phase II location tracking stand as a testament to our ability to adapt and improve. Now, when you dial 911 from your smartphone, you can rest assured that your call for help comes with a built-in GPS guide for first responders. It's a far cry from those early days when you might have had to resort to celestial navigation to describe your whereabouts.

Wireless 911 and Phase II location technology bridge the gap between the lost and the found, turning every cell signal into a beacon of hope.

RapidSOS and Prepared Live

In this ever-evolving world of emergency dispatching, two dynamic forces have joined forces to create a life-saving partnership that would make even superheroes envious. RapidSOS and Prepared Live, the dynamic duo, have come together to revolutionize how 911 dispatchers operate, showing a new era of public safety that can only be described as "out of this world."

RapidSOS, the brainchild of modern emergency response, has crafted the world's first emergency response data platform. This powerhouse securely connects life-saving data from a staggering 400 million+ connected devices to the fingertips of emergency services and first responders. They're like the central nervous system of emergency response, ensuring that vital information flows seamlessly when needed.

Along with data, RapidSOS is a champion "Where's Waldo" player. It has Apple and Google on speed dial. This dynamic duo teams up, transmitting your phone's location to 911 dispatchers through the RapidSOS Platform. How, you ask? Well, it's all about those little sensors that make your phone tick – GPS, WI-Fi, Bluetooth, and even barometric pressure. RapidSOS harnesses their power, transforming your device into a location-sending superhero.

On the other side of the equation, we have Prepared Live, a software solution developed by Prepared, dedicated to helping emergency dispatchers save lives. At its core, Prepared Live is a game-changer.

It empowers dispatchers to do the impossible: live streaming and receiving a treasure trove of multimedia – photos, videos, texts, and GPS locations – all in real-time. Dispatchers have been given a front-row seat to the unfolding emergency, armed with the information they need to make split-second decisions.

And the excitement doesn't stop there. RapidSOS and Prepared Live have teamed up, conjuring new features and functionalities to further save lives. One exciting project in the early stages is a first responder extension that promises seamless communication and data-sharing with those who are first on the scene.

In the ever-evolving world of public safety, RapidSOS and Prepared Live are leading the charge, pushing the boundaries of what's possible. They're not just partners; they're the driving force behind a safer, more connected future where every call for help is met with the speed, efficiency, and precision it deserves.

RapidSOS and Prepared Live join forces, turning real-time information into a lifeline, ensuring help arrives swiftly and prepared.

History Of CAD

The fascinating history of Computer-Aided Dispatch, or CAD, in the world of emergency dispatching – a tale of technological evolution that took us from the Stone Age of paper maps and rotary phones to the digital age of efficiency and precision.

In the prehistoric era of the 1960s, dispatch centers were reminiscent of a detective's office in a noir film. Then, in 1967, the concept of CAD was born as the Los Angeles Police Department took its first steps into the brave new world of computerized dispatching. Gone were the days of dispatchers deciphering handwritten notes and frantically spinning the wheel of rotary phones. It was the turning point where computers would lend a helping hand.

The 1970s brought us the first practical CAD system designed to streamline dispatch operations and reduce response times. Salt Lake City became the proud adopter of this revolutionary technology. Dispatchers could now breathe easy as they entered incident details into their computers, which magically matched available resources. No more tangled web of radio chatter; CAD was here to sort things out.

In 1981, New York City joined the CAD club, marking a momentous occasion. The Big Apple's dispatchers were no longer just using pencils and paper to manage their bustling metropolis; they had CAD at their fingertips. It was the decade of disco, and dispatchers danced to the rhythm of CAD's efficiency.

As we fast-forward to the new millennium, CAD systems have become indispensable tools in emergency dispatching. Today, dispatch centers across the globe rely on CAD to manage incidents, allocate resources, and provide the precise information first responders need. It's not just a tool; it's a lifeline.

In the evolution of dispatch, Computer-Aided Dispatch (CAD) is the orchestration of resources, turning chaos into coordinated response.

History Of Emergency Services Radios

E mergency services had a communication conundrum in a world without smartphones and emojis. They needed a way to talk to each other that was more advanced than smoke signals and tin cans connected by string.

Way back in the early 1900s, Marconi was making waves (radio waves, that is) with his groundbreaking wireless telegraphy. The first practical use of radios in emergency services took shape during World War I when military forces used radios to coordinate their efforts. The civilian world soon caught on, realizing that radios could be game-changing in emergencies.

In 1928, Detroit took the spotlight by becoming the first city to establish a centralized two-way radio system for police cars. The birth of the "Bat-Signal," but instead of calling Batman, it was for cops to tackle real-life villains.

As time marched on, the '40s and '50s saw the increase of two-way radios in police and fire departments across the United States. Not unlike kids with walkie-talkies, only with less playful banter and more "We've got a 10-13 at 5th and Main."

Then, in the '90s, public safety radio systems took a digital turn. Analog radios were out, and digital was in. The quality was crisper, like listening to your favorite '90s CD instead of a scratched-up vinyl record.

But no story about the evolution of emergency services radio systems would be complete without mentioning 9/11. The tragic events of September 11, 2001, exposed the shortcomings of the existing systems. Communication failures between first responders highlighted the need for interoperability – a fancy word meaning that different agencies and jurisdictions could talk to each other seamlessly.

In response, the U.S. government took action. They allocated billions of dollars to modernize and improve public safety radio systems. New standards were set, ensuring radios from different manufacturers could play nice together. It was like the emergency services' version of a playdate.

Today's world has advanced digital systems, trunked radio networks, and even encrypted communication. The future meets the present. Emergency services radio systems have come a long way from their humble beginnings. It's a far cry from the days of Marconi and his telegraphy. Still, it's a tale of progress and innovation that continues to evolve. Where technology and heroism collide in a world of codes, signals, and life-saving waves.

Through the crackling waves of time, emergency services radios have been the steady voice of courage, guiding heroes into the unknown.

Emergency Medical Dispatch (EMD)

I n the grand tapestry of emergency dispatching, a humble but critical thread exists known as Emergency Medical Dispatch (EMD). When facing a medical crisis, dial those three magic numbers – 911. But instead of waiting for help to arrive, you're greeted by a calm and knowledgeable voice on the other end, guiding you through the storm.

Let's hop in our time machine and return to the 1960s. It was a different era, where the internet was but a glimmer in some tech-savvy visionary's eye. During this time, emergency calls were more of a guessing game. You dialed 911, and the dispatcher on the other end did their best to determine what kind of emergency you were facing and which responders to send. It was like playing a game of charades but with lives on the line.

But then, in 1968, the heavens parted, and the concept of EMD was born. The key players in this life-saving revolution were the fire chiefs of Winnipeg, Canada, who recognized the need for a standardized system for handling medical emergencies. They devised a protocol that allowed dispatchers to send help and provide pre-arrival medical instructions.

Imagine the Eureka moment when they realized that dispatchers could do more than just pass along information; they could actually help save lives by guiding callers through CPR, stopping bleeding, or assisting with childbirth. Dispatchers suddenly became emergency room doctors with a direct line to your living room.

In the 1970s, the EMD concept started gaining traction in the United States. Thanks to the efforts of medical professionals, emergency responders, and communication experts, the first EMD programs were established. This was the era of pioneering, where protocols were created, training programs developed, and the role of the dispatcher evolved into something akin to a medical superhero.

Over the years, EMD has continued to evolve. Modern technology has allowed dispatchers to use sophisticated software for quick and accurate assessments. The goal is simple – to get the right help as fast as possible and equip you with the knowledge and skills to make a difference until help arrives.

If you face a medical emergency, when you dial 911, you're not just reaching out for help but connecting with a network of EMD heroes. They're the unsung saviors behind the scenes, armed with protocols, compassion, and a mission to guide you through the storm – one life-saving call at a time.

In the realm of medical emergencies, EMD dispatchers are the unseen heroes, providing life-saving guidance with unwavering dedication.

Emergency Alerts and Reverse 911

O nce upon a time, not too long ago, we didn't have the luxury of our smartphones blaring emergency alerts at us, startling us from TikTok and Snaps. Oh no, in those dark ages, we relied on the town crier, the siren's wail, or perhaps a strongly worded letter tied to a pigeon's leg. But fear not, for the advent of emergency alert systems has since brought us into the modern age of mass notifications.

Our journey begins in the not-so-distant past, the 1950s, during the Cold War period when the threat of nuclear annihilation loomed like a rain cloud over a picnic. The Civil Defense program answered this imminent peril, introducing sirens and public service announcements to warn folks about potential atomic Armageddon. Imagine the joy of hearing that screeching siren, knowing you had just moments to seek shelter or kiss your picnic goodbye!

Then, the 1990s arrived, and with them, the advent of Emergency Alert System (EAS) technology. This system was designed to replace the old Emergency Broadcast System (EBS), which, let's face it, was about as efficient as sending a telegram via horse and buggy. The EAS allowed authorities to send warnings via broadcast stations, cable systems, and, eventually, the internet. The beauty of it? You could be in the middle of binge-watching your favorite '90s sitcom, and suddenly, that show would be interrupted by a stern voice warning you of impending doom. How's that for a plot twist?

But wait, there's more! Enter the Reverse 911, a technology that turned the tables on how we notify the masses. It emerged in the early 2000s, and the concept was simple. Instead of authorities broadcasting messages to everyone, they could target specific areas or individuals with crucial information. Imagine the relief of not receiving a tornado warning when you live in the desert.

But Reverse 911 isn't just about weathering storms. It's a versatile tool in the emergency notification arsenal. This technology has proven invaluable, from wildfire evacuations to hazardous material spill warnings.

Now, as we bask in the generation of smartphones and smartwatches, emergency alert systems have become a part of our daily lives. They've evolved to deliver information about weather emergencies, Amber Alerts, public safety alerts, and even presidential alerts. Yep, the President can send you a message that will light up your screen and perhaps your life with a mix of surprise and concern.

While we may look back and chuckle at the days of pigeon-delivered letters and town criers, we must also tip our hats to the evolution of emergency alert systems. They've come a long way, ensuring that in times of crisis, whether man-made or natural, you'll be well-informed, even if it occasionally interrupts your binge-watching session.

In the age of instant communication, emergency alerts and Reverse 911 empower communities to stand strong in the face of adversity.

II

Criminal Shenanigans and Corrections

Step gingerly into the world of criminal shenanigans and corrections, where handcuffs are more than just a fashion statement, prison escapes could put Hollywood to shame, and correctional slang is a language more cryptic than a treasure map's riddle. 'Criminal Shenanigans and Corrections' is your ticket to exploring the wild, weird, and occasionally wacky moments in the annals of criminal justice. Get ready to laugh, gasp, and wonder how on earth we ever managed to keep the bad guys behind bars.

History of Corrections

O nce upon a time, in a world not so far away, the history of corrections was being etched into the stone walls of primitive societies. It's a tale as old as time, where people grappled with the age-old question: What do we do with those who break the rules?

Long before orange jumpsuits and barbed wire fences, ancient civilizations were pioneers of the penitentiary. Take ancient Rome, for instance. The Romans, ever the trendsetters, had their "carcer" – a dank dungeon where wrongdoers awaited their fate. It was a place where prisoners were treated like celebrities – if, you know, celebrities were chained to walls and surrounded by rats.

Then, the Middle Ages. Ah, yes, castles, knights, and... dungeons. Castles doubled as makeshift correctional facilities, with chambers so dark and damp that even the rats filed formal complaints. Prisoners spent their days rotting away, pondering their misdeeds and wishing for central heating.

Fast-tracking a bit, and behold the birth of the workhouse. It was a delightful institution where those who dared to be poor were sentenced to hard labor and gruel. It was basically a vacation package that combined the charm of prison life with the ambiance of a Dickensian novel.

Of course, no history of corrections is complete without a nod to the picturesque galleys of yore. A floating paradise where convicts rowed their way to glory. It blended cardio and punishment perfectly, set against stunning sea vistas and the occasional pirate raid.

Now, don't let your heart sink – the modern era brought its own innovations. The birth of the panopticon, the brainchild of Jeremy Bentham. This architectural marvel was the Mona Lisa of prisons – where guards constantly watched prisoners from a central watchtower. It was like a real-life reality show with drama, suspense, and limited bathroom breaks.

And then came the era of the penitentiary. No, it is not a place to perfect your penmanship but a haven for self-reflection and rehabilitation. It was here that the concept of solitary confinement was born. Because what better way to reform someone than by locking them up with their thoughts 24/7? Who needs social interaction if you can have introspective breakdowns instead?

Moving into the industrial revolution, and voilà – the birth of the modern prison complex. With factories on the rise and labor in high demand, what better way to kill two birds with one stone than by forcing inmates to toil away in the name of progress? Indeed, a match made in heaven – or at least in some smoke-filled factory somewhere.

Scrolling through history, we arrive at the 20th century, when the "big house" era was in full swing. Complete with iron bars, armed guards, and cafeteria food that could double as construction material, the big house embodied tough love. Because, after all, nothing says rehabilitation like sharing a cell with folks who've perfected the art of cat burglary.

There you have it, a whirlwind story through the history of corrections – a saga of dungeons, toil, and the noble pursuit of making bad guys better. From ancient dungeons to modern penitentiaries, the evolution of corrections is a tale of creativity, innovation, and a dash of irony that will leave you wondering: Have we truly progressed, or are we just serving time in a different kind of cell?

The history of corrections is a chronicle of society's efforts to manage its darker impulses, a testament to our ever-evolving pursuit of justice.

Famous Inmates

In the world of fame and folly, even the most glittering stars couldn't escape the clutches of correctional facilities. Behold the intriguing tales of famous inmates who temporarily traded their red carpets for concrete walls and metal bars. Get ready to journey through the hallowed halls of celebrity incarceration, where headlines collide with handcuffs.

Al Capone, the legendary gangster with a penchant for pinstripes and prohibition, found himself in Alcatraz – the rock-hard, inescapable fortress that turned even the most cunning minds into mere mortals. Capone's glittering empire crumbled, and he became inmate number 85 to remind everyone that even the biggest fish can be reeled in.

Next, there was Martha Stewart – the queen of homemaking who turned insider trading into an art form. As she embarked on her quest through the prison system, you can't help but wonder if she offered tips on how to fold fitted sheets with that signature smile. "Ladies and gentlemen, today's lesson is on how to make the perfect prison potpourri using just three contraband items."

But wait, it's not just the mobsters and homemakers who graced the corridors of correctional facilities. The musical maestro, Johnny Cash, famously sang about the Folsom Prison Blues – guess what? He performed live for the inmates at Folsom State Prison itself. Talk about the ultimate fan service. "Hello, inmates! Hope you're all having a good time in this place I've heard so much about."

Remember Lindsay Lohan? The poster child for celebrity drama? She danced her way into a brief stay at the Lynwood Correctional Facility. It was like a reality TV crossover – where rehab meets incarceration in a spectacular mess that would baffle even the most seasoned producers.

But who could forget the dynamic duo of Nick Nolte and his unforgettable mugshot? Nolte's disheveled hair and bemused expression earned him a spot in the Hall of Fame of celebrity booking photos. It was as if he was auditioning for the "disheveled yet charming inmate" role in a Hollywood blockbuster.

And the high priest of hip-hop, Snoop Dogg. The rapper's brush with the law wasn't just a cameo but a full-blown performance at the Hilton. The irony of "Drop It Like It's Hot" echoing through prison halls is a testament to life's sense of humor.

Speaking of humor, even the ever-suave George Clooney had his moment behind bars. It wasn't method acting for a blockbuster but a protest against the Sudanese embassy. And yes, even Hollywood's leading man had to endure a night in the slammer for standing up for what he believed in.

The journey through these tales of celebrity incarceration is a reminder that fame and fortune don't come with immunity from the long arm of the law. From Alcatraz to Lynwood, even the most illustrious names have found themselves in the company of guards and cells, trading autographs for inmate numbers.

A peek behind the velvet ropes of celebrity confinement. It turns out that even amidst the glitz and glamour, there's always room for a little orange jumpsuit chic. After all, who needs a red carpet when you can strut your stuff down the cell block runway?

Behind the walls of prisons, even the most famous of men are reduced to mere numbers, their stories hidden in the shadows.

Prison Escapes

In the domain of audacity and desperation, the saga of prison escapes unfolds – a mesmerizing dance of cunning and courage. Prepare to be captivated by the tales of inmates who defied bars and boundaries, proving that even the most robust walls can't contain the human spirit.

Frank Abagnale – a con artist extraordinaire who spun the art of deception into a daring escape from a federal detention center. With a dash of charisma and a sprinkle of forgery, Abagnale pulled off a bold feat that left authorities scratching their heads and his fellow inmates wondering if they should've paid closer attention in art class.

This escapade, which could easily double as a script for an action-comedy film, involved Abagnale using his charm and cunning to impersonate an undercover prison inspector. Successfully convincing the guards that he was, in fact, an authority figure rather than an inmate, he cunningly secured his release. It's almost as if Abagnale took inspiration from a magician's handbook, substituting rabbits and doves for legal documents and impersonations.

But wait, there's more. In a "life imitating art case," three inmates escaped Alcatraz, the supposedly impenetrable fortress of isolation. They concocted an ingenious plan involving a makeshift raft fashioned from raincoats and some cardboard boxes. If this doesn't scream "survival of the fittest," then I don't know what does.

Then there's the unforgettable tale of Pascal Payet – the French daredevil who staged not one but two helicopter escapes from prisons. He practically elevated the term "getaway vehicle" to new heights. It's almost as if he whispered to the wind, "Why break out the old-fashioned way when you can take the scenic route?"

The Houdinis' of the prison world – those who mastered the art of tunneling. One inmate in Mexico managed to dig a tunnel from his cell to the outside world. You have to admire the dedication – it's not every day you get to combine fitness and freedom in one ingenious endeavor.

But the creativity continues beyond there. Inmates have been known to master the art of disguise – some daring enough to dress up as correctional officers, complete with uniforms and badges. It is a real-life game of cops and robbers, where the lines between the two blur in a display of chutzpah.

Then there's the tale of the infamous El Chapo, who engineered not one but two jailbreaks. The first involved a laundry cart that would make any dry cleaner proud. And the second? A brazen escape on a motorbike through a tunnel beneath his prison cell. If you're going to break out, you might as well make it a grand spectacle, right?

Of course, the age-old trick of "playing dead" has also appeared. Inmates have been known to feign illness or even death to secure a spot outside prison walls. It's a plot twist worthy of a Hollywood screenplay – if only they could've gotten a cameo by the Grim Reaper.

As we waltz through these tales of prison escapades, it's clear that human ingenuity knows no bounds. From tunnels to raincoat rafts, disguises to deception, these stories remind us that where there's a will, there's a way – even if that way involves some questionable DIY skills and a whole lot of audacity.

In the world of prison, where the walls are high and the guards are many, the art of escape becomes the poetry of freedom.

Infamous Prisons

A rogues' gallery of notorious prisons lies in the shadowy corners of the world, where steel bars and locked gates reign supreme. These penal institutions are more than just brick and mortar; they're the stuff of legends, where stories of daring escapes, brutal regimes, and inmates' creative attempts at freedom take center stage.

First on the tour is Alcatraz – the rock-hard fortress more famous for its impossible escapes than its ocean views. In the chilly waters of San Francisco Bay, Alcatraz held some of the most notorious criminals in the United States. The island's nickname, "The Rock," sounds more like a trendy nightclub, but make no mistake, this place was where dreams of freedom were swiftly sunk.

Now, venturing to Devil's Island in French Guiana – a place that sounds like it was designed by a horror movie set decorator. This remote island prison was a living nightmare, where inmates were shipped to serve sentences in a hellish jungle environment. Forget orange jumpsuits; here, prisoners sported the classic "sweat-soaked rags" ensemble, courtesy of Mother Nature.

And who could forget Robben Island off the coast of South Africa? This institution gained infamy as the prison where Nelson Mandela spent 18 years. It's like a real-life superhero origin story – minus the capes and comic book villains. The crushing regime aimed to break the spirits of inmates, but instead, it fueled a fire that would change the world.

Altiplano Federal Penitentiary, the home of El Chapo's infamous escapes. This subterranean tunnel masterpiece puts your weekend DIY projects to shame. This mile-long tunnel under the penitentiary in Mexico had lighting, ventilation, and a motorcycle track for a grand exit. It was like a twisted version of Disneyland's Space Mountain, with a much higher risk of life imprisonment.

Then, we have the notorious Bang Kwang Central Prison in Thailand. This place has the charming nickname "Bangkok Hilton." The "Hilton" experience here is far from luxurious; it's a stark reminder that real life rarely imitates glossy brochures. Inmates wear uniforms that could double as overalls for a medieval blacksmith, which adds a certain charm to their stay.

Let's not forget Rikers Island in New York City – a place so infamous that it practically has its own zip code in pop culture. Known for its grim reputation and a revolving door of characters, Rikers Island is like a reality TV show with incredibly high stakes. It's not just a prison; it's an ongoing drama with a cast of thousands.

And who could overlook the Tower of London? This historical fortress has witnessed centuries of imprisonment, execution, and intrigue. Its tales of imprisoned royalty, alleged witches, and political dissidents make it a hotspot for history buffs and ghost enthusiasts alike. You might say it's the original reality show set, complete with a moat and a few resident ravens.

One thing becomes clear as we venture through these notorious prisons: their histories blend tragedy, defiance, and the indomitable human spirit. From El Chapo's tunnel to the Tower of London's chilling cells, these institutions remind us that the human capacity for survival, even in the darkest of places, knows no bounds.

A whirlwind tour through infamy and incarceration. Whether escaping the inescapable, enduring brutal regimes or embracing the legends surrounding them, these prisons have left an indelible mark on history.

And who knows, maybe they'll add guided tours and souvenir shops to their repertoire one day.

Infamous prisons stand as silent witnesses to the human capacity for cruelty and the enduring quest for redemption.

Correctional Slang

B ehind the iron bars and drab walls of correctional facilities lies a world not just of confinement but also of its very own dictionary. Yes, my dear language enthusiasts, it's time to delve into the colorful and oh-so-inventive kingdom of correctional slang. Just when you thought you had enough slang to decipher in the outside world, inmates have created their own linguistic playground within prison walls.

You might be thinking, "Wait, they have their own language in there?" Oh, indeed, they do. A parallel universe where "cellphone" isn't a device but a rather poetic term for a homemade knife, and "chow" doesn't signify a hearty meal at a fancy restaurant but is simply prison food, if you can call it that. It's almost like they took Scrabble tiles with words and meanings and tossed them up in the air just to see what would stick.

When inmates enter the correctional universe, they're bombarded with a barrage of new words that are as unique as the tattoos that adorn their bodies. "Fish" is not an underwater creature here, but a fresh inmate swimming in the prison pond for the first time. And if you ever hear the word "crumb" being tossed around, don't worry—it's not about the culinary arts. It's simply a term for a minor infraction that, let's face it, might as well be called a "tiny bite of rule-breaking."

Now, "kites," and no, they're not colorful, soaring objects in the sky. Inmates refer to written messages passed surreptitiously between cells as kites as if their letters are floating effortlessly on the prison breeze. And just when you think you've mastered the slang, someone drops the "Green Balloon" term. No, it's not a new party game—it's code for a package from home because what says "I care" more than sending a loved one a... green balloon?

But perhaps one of the most creative forms of prison slang is the use of seemingly innocent words with entirely new meanings. "Cheese" doesn't mean dairy delight here—it's money. And if someone asks you about the "iron," don't start searching for a clothes press. They're referring to the concrete bars that separate them from the outside world, and probably the iron will, too.

Correctional slang is more than just a hodgepodge of words—it's a culture, a way of life, and a way to communicate in a world where freedom is limited. While we may chuckle at the audacity of some of these terms, we must recognize that they serve a deeper purpose— connecting people who find themselves confined and creating a sense of community in the unlikeliest places.

There you have it, dear language aficionados. The quirky, witty, and sometimes downright baffling world of correctional slang. It's a reminder that even in the most challenging circumstances, humans have a knack for inventing language that's as resilient and inventive as they are. Now, if you'll excuse me, I think I've just about mastered the basics, and I'm ready to join the "slang party," even if it's just from the comfort of my wordy armchair.

Within the language of incarceration, slang becomes a dialect of survival, a secret code in a world apart.

Unusual Contraband

In the "What Were They Thinking," world prison contraband takes a curious turn. Inmates, those masters of innovation and audacity, have elevated smuggling to an art form – and the results are nothing short of baffling. Prepare to be amazed, bewildered, and perhaps slightly concerned as we look into the world of unusual contraband confiscated from behind bars.

First, talk about the humble pigeon – the original avian smuggler. In a plot straight out of a cartoon caper, inmates attempted to use carrier pigeons to ferry drugs and other goodies into the prison. If only these pigeons could've been trained in the art of discreet drop-offs instead of conspicuous landings on prison windowsills.

A cute, fluffy kitten. You'd expect it to be the harbinger of cuddles, right? Well, not in contraband. In one case, a kitten was discovered with a tiny backpack full of illegal substances. It resembles a bizarre version of "bring your pet to work day," except the pet is a criminal accomplice.

But why stop at furry creatures? Inmates have been known to use drones to deliver contraband, turning the prison yard into a makeshift landing pad for technological feats. It's a bit like Amazon Prime, except instead of ordering toilet paper, you're requesting illicit substances with a side of audacity.

And then there are the inventive approaches to smuggling that rival the world's most perplexing riddle. From hollowed-out books to secret compartments in shoes, it's as if inmates are participating in a real-life game of "hide and seek" with prison guards. If only they could've used these skills in a more legal profession.

But the creativity doesn't stop there. One inmate attempted to smuggle contraband inside a prosthetic leg. Yes, you read that correctly – a prosthetic leg. This is similar to a twisted version of "Legends of the Hidden Temple," where the prize is more jail time and less glory.

And the case of a potato... – not your average spud, mind you. This potato was hollowed out to house a mobile phone. It's the kind of innovation that would make even the most resourceful potato farmer raise an eyebrow. Who knew that starchy vegetables could moonlight as cell phones?

But perhaps the most astonishing case involves a mannequin. Used to smuggle contraband out of a prison. It resembles a prison break starring the cast of a department store's display window. If only mannequins could be charged with aiding and abetting – they'd certainly have some explaining to do.

As we wade through the sea of baffling contraband cases, it's clear that inmates possess an uncanny ability to turn everyday objects into smuggling vehicles. From drones to kittens to mannequins, these cases remind us that when it comes to creativity, inmates are in a league of their own. Who knew that the world of contraband would be such a treasure trove of audacious antics and bizarre choices?

So there you have it – a voyage through the world of unusual contraband that leaves us equal parts amused and flabbergasted. From pigeons with hidden agendas to potatoes with secret lives, these stories showcase the lengths inmates will go to in their quest for forbidden treasures.

In the realm of contraband, the imagination knows no bounds,
as everyday objects become tools of defiance and creativity.

Prison Riots

A h, the musical symphony of chaos, where the clashing notes of anger and frustration crescendo into a full-blown riot. Yes, I'm talking about those infamous episodes of mayhem that occur within the hallowed halls of prisons—prison riots, to be exact. It's almost like a twisted form of team-building, where inmates bond over their shared discontent and decide to redecorate their living space with a touch of anarchy.

It is a seemingly average day in the life of a correctional facility, where inmates are going about their usual routines of monotony and confinement. But suddenly, something sparks like a lightning bolt from the skies of rebellion. Maybe it's the unappetizing "mystery meat" at lunch or the realization that orange isn't a flattering color on anyone. Whatever it is, it's enough to set the stage for a grand production, a riot of epic proportions.

These riots are like the rebellious offspring of a prison's population, demonstrating their mastery of creative expression, albeit in a destructive manner. Furniture is upturned, windows are shattered, and let's not forget the ever-ingenious makeshift weapons that appear out of thin air—because what's a riot without a few impromptu spears and clubs? It's a real-life version of "Lord of the Flies," only with a more confined set and less conch-shell symbolism.

One of the most celebrated riots in these impromptu theatrics occurred in Attica Correctional Facility in 1971. Inmates united under the banner of change, demanding better living conditions and fundamental human rights. Their demands were met with what can only be described as a highly effective negotiation strategy involving tear gas and live ammunition. The final act left dozens dead and hundreds injured, proving that sometimes, even the most earnest efforts to bring about change can spiral into chaos.

Then there's the New Mexico State Penitentiary Riot of 1980, where inmates took control of the prison and staged a little avant-garde performance involving fire, murder, and general mayhem. The end result was a grand spectacle of destruction, showcasing the inmates' penchant for theatrical pyrotechnics.

Not to be overlooked is the notorious Lucasville Prison Riot of 1993, which, like any good show, had an ensemble cast of inmates from different gangs. Their collaborative efforts resulted in a lengthy hostage situation, fatalities, and a general sense of bedlam. It's almost as if they were auditioning for the role of "Anarchist of the Year."

Ultimately, these prison riots are more than just moments of chaos—they showcase the human desire for change, even if it comes in shattered glass and charred remains. Whether it's Attica, New Mexico, or Lucasville, these events have carved their place in the annals of history, reminding us that sometimes, the inmates are the ones who get to have the last word, even if it's in a language of rebellion and destruction.

When despair ignites, the flames of revolution roar within prison walls, a stark reminder of the power of the human spirit.

Death Row Procedures

L adies and gentlemen, prepare for a tale as old as time—well, at least as old as the concept of civilization itself. We're delving into the riveting history of the death penalty, a practice that's been around since the dawn of "an eye for an eye" became a catchy slogan.

A caveman clubbing another caveman over the head for swiping his favorite saber-toothed tiger skin. Fast forward a bit, and we find ourselves in ancient Babylon, where Hammurabi's Code casually included death as a solution for various offenses. Talk about a no-nonsense legal system.

As the centuries passed, the death penalty became the go-to solution for all sorts of societal issues. Witchcraft? Off with her head! Stealing a loaf of bread? Prepare the guillotine! And delightful public executions—the ultimate in crowd-pleasing entertainment.

Fast-forward to the present day, where the death penalty has become a high-stakes game of legal ping-pong. The procedures are like a well-rehearsed dance routine, complete with appeals, last-minute stays, and enough paperwork to choke a horse. It's reminiscent of trying to order at a fast-food joint during the lunch rush—confusing, frustrating, and prone to numerous delays.

The methods of execution have certainly evolved from the days of hangings and beheadings. We've got lethal injections, gas chambers, and even the electric chair, all designed to ensure a "humane" exit from this mortal coil. Because nothing says "humane" quite like deliberately ending someone's life.

But wait, there's more! The death penalty has become a topic of heated debate, pitting the "eye for an eye" crowd against those pesky human rights advocates. Reminiscent of a showdown between medieval morality and modern sensibilities, with each side brandishing their arguments like swords in a duel.

Then there's the classic case of mistaken identity. There have been instances where the wrong person was nearly executed, proving that even the most meticulous legal systems can make glaring errors. But hey, who doesn't love a good game of legal roulette?

As we look deeper into the death penalty's history, we uncover layers of societal ethics and moral quandaries. Is it really justice, or just a masquerade of retribution dressed up in a fancy legal gown? Does it deter crime or simply satisfy a primitive thirst for vengeance?

In the end, the history of the death penalty is a roller coaster of shifting attitudes, questionable procedures, and the eternal struggle between justice and mercy. It's a tale as old as time, with its fair share of drama, controversy, and a dash of dark humor. As we bid adieu to this chapter in the annals of human history, let's raise a metaphorical glass to the evolution of punishment and the unending quest to find the balance between right and wrong, vengeance and compassion. Cheers—or should we say, "to death and back again."

In the solemn corridors of death row, the machinery of justice grinds slowly, while the weight of finality hangs heavy in the air.

Prison Architecture

P repare to be imprisoned in the captivating history of prison architecture, a tale of walls, bars, and innovative ways to keep miscreants from wandering off. From the ancient dungeons to the modern-day correctional facilities, the evolution of prison design has been a masterclass in mixing functionality with the occasional flair for the dramatic.

In medieval times, dungeons were all the rage—dark, dank, and just a tad claustrophobic. Because nothing says "rehabilitation" like locking someone in a dimly lit cell with chains and rats as companions. But hey, at least they were effective at preventing escape unless you happened to have a magic ring and a dwarf friend.

Fast-forward a few centuries, and voilà! We've got panopticons— essentially, the Big Brother of the architectural world. These circular designs allowed a single watchman to keep an eye on all the inmates simultaneously, proving once and for all that surveillance isn't just for reality TV.

Then came the "modern" prison era, with its cookie-cutter cell blocks and efficient designs. Nothing says "reform" like rows upon rows of identical cells, where inmates can bond over the color scheme and the charming view of a brick wall. Who needs windows when you've got fluorescent lighting?

But wait, the fun doesn't stop there! The 19th century brought us the birth of the panopticon's rebellious cousin—the radial design. A prison in the shape of a starfish, with cell blocks emanating from a central hub. It's on par with a penitentiary version of a pinwheel, with inmates spinning merrily in their cells. Who knew incarceration could be so whimsical?

As the years rolled on, architects continued experimenting with designs that best blended the dual purposes of punishment and rehabilitation. There were architectural competitions, brainstorming sessions, and countless blueprints that aimed to find that elusive sweet spot between humane conditions and, well, incarceration.

Modern prison architecture, as seen in supermax facilities, is like a fortress designed by an OCD perfectionist. High walls, layers of security, and enough surveillance cameras to make George Orwell blush. When it comes to keeping inmates in, nothing expresses "stay put" like a 20-foot concrete wall topped with razor wire.

Nowadays, prison architects face the challenge of creating environments that promote rehabilitation while still adhering to the security measures that keep Houdini-wannabes at bay. It's a delicate balance, like serving a soufflé in a straitjacket.

The history of prison architecture is a tale of innovation, experimentation, and the occasional architectural whimsy. From the dank dungeons to the sleek supermax facilities, each design choice reflects the prevailing attitudes toward punishment, reform, and the delicate dance between security and humanity.

Prison architecture mirrors the evolution of society's values, a reflection of our beliefs in punishment, reform, and the pursuit of justice.

Historical Landmarks

When "making lemonade out of lemons," former prisons have undergone a transformation that's as surprising as it is paradoxical. These once-dreaded correctional institutions have traded their roles as houses of confinement for a new gig – historical landmarks and tourist hotspots.

First, we have Alcatraz – the notorious island penitentiary that's like a magnet for history buffs and adventure seekers alike. It's as if the world collectively decided that an island once synonymous with despair could become a must-visit destination. Now, tourists line up to experience the eerie silence of the cell blocks, taking selfies in the very spots where inmates once dreamt of escape.

But Alcatraz is just the tip of the iceberg. Eastern State Penitentiary, a place that's gone from a fortress of punishment to a historical treasure trove. The crumbling cell blocks and eerie atmosphere provide the perfect backdrop for those seeking a dash of darkness while sightseeing. It's like an unconventional theme park, where the roller coasters are the tales of inmates' struggles, and the souvenir shops sell entirely different merchandise.

Not to be forgotten, Robben Island – a former prison turned UNESCO World Heritage Site that has witnessed both Nelson Mandela's incarceration and his triumph. Visitors can see the resilience of the human spirit through its heart-wrenching yet inspiring history.

Of course, the trend is broader than islands and crumbling cell blocks. San Pedro Prison in Bolivia offers guided tours, attracting tourists who want to glimpse into its world. Similar to a reality TV show where the cameras are swapped for curious travelers armed with cameras and questions.

And then there's Kilmainham Gaol in Ireland – a place that once housed political prisoners and now welcomes visitors eager to explore its dark history. The halls seem haunted by ghosts, a reminder of the struggles and sacrifices that led to the nation's independence.

But the cherry on top of this peculiar trend is the Old Melbourne Gaol. This former prison serves up a dose of history and spookiness in equal measure. Not unlike a haunted house on steroids, where visitors can tour the mysterious cells and even stand on the exact spot where Australia's most famous outlaw, Ned Kelly, met his doom.

Exploring these former prisons turned historical landmarks, one thing becomes clear: the line between punishment and preservation can be surprisingly thin. These sites have embraced their pasts, offering visitors a chance to reflect on the struggles of those who once walked their halls. From Alcatraz to Robben Island, these landmarks remind us that history is more complex and intriguing than we could ever think.

Historical landmarks in corrections are reminders of our collective journey, where bricks and bars bear witness to the changing tides of penology.

III

Law Enforcement Legends

Behold, the world of law enforcement, where officers in uniform are the tip of the spear in the battle against chaos, where K-9 units outsmart the most intelligent criminals, and where reading Miranda Rights sometimes feels like playing a game of 'Simon says' with high stakes. In 'Law Enforcement Legends,' we're about to embark on a journey filled with bizarre cases, unexpected twists, and a healthy dose of humor. Strap in because crime never looked so entertaining.

K-9 Units

G et ready to unleash your curiosity on the fascinating history of police K-9 units, where our four-legged furry friends went from being mere companions to the ultimate crime-fighting sidekicks. A tail-wagging tale of sniffing out trouble and catching criminals, all while maintaining an air of undeniable cuteness.

The story begins in the early 20th century when some bright mind thought, "Hey, wouldn't it be cool if we added dogs to our law enforcement team?" Thus, police K-9 units were born, with the inaugural members probably sporting monocles and tiny detective hats. These early dogs must have been pioneers, braving the uncharted territory of police work while still mastering the art of fetch.

Soon, police departments realized that dogs had an uncanny knack for using their superior sense of smell to track down even the sneakiest of criminals. "Scent discrimination" became their middle name, and suddenly, Lassie had some serious competition in the heroism department.

As the years passed, police dogs graduated from occasional helpers to full-fledged force members. They were no longer just "assistants" but partners, comrades, and possibly even the reason behind the phrase "man's best friend." These K-9 officers were trained to detect drugs and explosives and even locate missing persons while looking remarkably cute in their custom-designed vests.

Then, police dogs became celebrities in their own right. They starred in action-packed movies and T.V. shows, showing their impeccable obedience and knack for taking down bad guys. Move over, human actors—these furry performers were stealing the show, one bark at a time.

Of course, no story is complete without a nod to the many different breeds of the K-9 unit. German Shepherds, Belgian Malinois, and Labrador Retrievers—each breed brought its unique skills to the table, whether it was agility, strength, or the power to melt hearts with a single wag.

In the modern era, police K-9 units are integral to law enforcement, demonstrating that you don't need a badge to be a hero. These dogs are trained rigorously, showcasing feats of bravery that would make even the most daring human officer pause in admiration. From taking down suspects to locating evidence, they do it all without the need for handcuffs or a Miranda warning.

From their humble beginnings as crime-fighting novelties to their present-day status as indispensable members of law enforcement, these furry officers have left paw prints on the hearts of officers and citizens alike. Whether they're sniffing out drugs, performing tricks for school children, or simply brightening up the precinct with their wagging tails, police dogs continue to show us that courage comes in all shapes, sizes, and fur coats.

In the paws of a loyal partner, courage takes a new form, and the bond between officer and K-9 is unbreakable.

Police History

L aw enforcement agencies have a colorful history in the grand theater of maintaining order. From the dawn of civilization to the digital age, the evolution of policing has seen it all – from loincloths to body cams and everything in between.

Starting at the beginning – ancient societies where the "long arm of the law" was more like a "short club of authority." In these primitive times, leaders relied on brute strength and a keen eye for troublemakers. Crime prevention was less about detective work and more about flexing muscles. "Stop in the name of club!" has a certain ring to it, don't you think?

Moving on to ancient Rome, where the Cohortes Urbanae was the precursor to modern policing. These early enforcers patrolled the bustling streets, dealing with everything from pickpockets to rowdy chariot drivers. Comparable to a time-traveling buddy cop movie, where toga-wearing officers rode chariots instead of squad cars.

The Wild West, where lawmen like Wyatt Earp and Bat Masterson faced off against outlaws in dusty towns straight out of a Hollywood Western. You can see it: sheriffs in ten-gallon hats and spurs, sauntering down Main Street, ready to dispense justice faster than you can say "draw!"

During the age of professionalism birthed the modern police forces in the 19th century. Sir Robert Peel's Metropolitan Police Service in London paved the way for the "bobbies" – those friendly officers who patrolled the streets with a sense of decorum and a healthy dose of skepticism. They were the O.G. influencers, setting the standards for law enforcement style and mannerisms.

As time marched on, so did technology. The era of the radio call and two-way communication systems allowed officers to coordinate like a well-choreographed dance routine. The police force embraced the art of teamwork while trading their dance shoes for badge-adorned uniforms.

Following that came the digital age – when police work wasn't just about beating the pavement but navigating the virtual world. Cybercrime units emerged, dealing with hackers and digital miscreants. A techno-thriller where the heroes wear badges and wield laptops instead of guns.

But the evolution of law enforcement isn't without its quirks. In the world of uniforms, we've seen everything from bowler hats to kevlar vests, depending on the fashion trends and the threats du jour. It's a game of dress-up where officers go from fashion-forward to full-on tactical in the blink of an eye.

And let's not overlook the occasional buddy cop partnership – real-life bromances that have the chemistry of a Hollywood blockbuster. Think Riggs and Murtaugh, only with fewer explosions and more paperwork.

While traversing the winding road of police history, one thing becomes clear: from club-wielding enforcers to cybercrime sleuths, the world of law enforcement has evolved in ways that could make even the most imaginative storytellers raise an eyebrow. The ride has been anything but boring from ancient Rome to the digital age. And as long as there are rules to be upheld and justice to be served, the story of police history will continue to evolve, one crime at a time.

The history of policing is a testament to our commitment to uphold justice, evolving through the ages to protect and serve.

Police Vehicles

Buckle up because we're about to ride through the bumpy history of police vehicles, where flashing lights and sirens meet some seriously questionable fashion choices.

Back in the early 20th century, police vehicles were like the distant relatives of modern cruisers. A clunky, black Ford Model T with a single, tiny red light on top, looking more like a lost firefly than a crime-fighting machine. But hey, it got the job done—albeit at the speed of a particularly determined tortoise.

Fast forward a bit, and the 1950s rolled in with some stylish offerings, like the Chevy Bel Air. Its sleek curves and chrome accents were like the James Bond of police cars. Okay, maybe not exactly, but it did have a certain charm that turned heads while chasing down speeders.

The 1970s were a wild time, and police vehicles decided to embrace their inner disco divas. The Ford Pinto police cruiser joined the scene, proving that even a compact car could look like it meant business. Of course, the mullets and bell bottoms only added to the ambiance.

But it was the 1980s that truly brought the "bling" to police rides. The Crown Victoria, affectionately known as the "Crown Vic," became the poster child for law enforcement vehicles. Decked out with oversized bumpers that screamed, "I'm here to party and arrest bad guys," the Crown Vic was the equivalent of an action hero in four-wheeled form.

As technology advanced, so did police vehicles. In the 1990s, the Ford

Explorer Police Interceptor prowled the streets, combining rugged SUV capabilities with a dash of intimidation. Picture a mighty cowboy riding into town. Only this cowboy wears a badge and drives a mean-looking SUV.

Not to be forgotten, the muscle cars that graced police fleets—yes, you read that right. The Dodge Charger Police Pursuit, a modern-day tribute to the muscle car era, proved that officers could be both enforcers of the law and enthusiasts of speed.

Today, police vehicles are equipped with all the bells and whistles (literally). They're practically rolling command centers from state-of-the-art communication systems to built-in laptops and advanced surveillance technology. And those classic red and blue lights have been joined by high-intensity LEDs that can signal an emergency from space—or at least from the other side of town.

In recent years, police departments have even dabbled in electric vehicles. Yes, silent and green, these cars prove that even law enforcement can have a touch of eco-friendliness. But let's be honest, nothing says "pull over" quite like the roaring engine of a traditional cruiser.

The wild and sometimes amusing evolution of police vehicles. These cars have seen everything from fireflies on wheels to sleek cruisers that command respect. They've chased down villains, patrolled neighborhoods, and provided a platform for officers to channel their inner action heroes. And who knows what the future holds? Maybe someday, police vehicles will come equipped with jet packs or hover technology. But until then, embrace the classic cruisers that have kept our streets safe, one siren-blaring chase at a time.

In the pursuit of justice, our vehicles become the steeds of duty, carrying officers into the heart of the unknown.

Miranda Rights

I t's the 1960s, and suspects facing police interrogations were similar to helpless figures in a suspenseful drama. Their words were weaponized against them without a second thought. But fear not, justice had its own script to rewrite in 1966.

Ernesto Miranda, an unsuspecting protagonist in this legal saga, was in a tight spot during police questioning. Little did he know that his ordeal would transform criminal rights forever. The Supreme Court, in a landmark decision, handed down the "Miranda v. Arizona" verdict, introducing the groundbreaking concept of Miranda warnings.

With the Miranda warning as the protagonist, the legal narrative took a dramatic turn. Now, when an individual is arrested and faces the impending interrogation, they hear the iconic lines: "You have the right to remain silent. Anything you say can and will be used against you in a court of law. You have the right to an attorney..." This phrase became ingrained in the legal lexicon, a testament to the enduring impact of this ruling.

Attorneys, legal scholars, and judicial minds engaged in heated debates over the precise verbiage of the warning. Should suspects explicitly be told they have the "right to an attorney present during questioning"? Or would a vague reference to the "right to counsel" suffice? These questions added layers of complexity to an already intriguing narrative.

Of course, some always aim to twist the narrative in their favor. Thus, "The Miranda Card," a fascinating subplot in this legal drama. Some individuals, believing they're legal maestros, invoke their Miranda rights in situations where they don't exactly apply. Imagine the neighbor who "remains silent" during a heated debate over missing garden tools—indeed, a comedic twist.

Miranda warnings became synonymous with legal dramas as the legal saga continued, inspiring countless T.V. shows, movies, and comedy sketches. From gripping courtroom scenes to humorous parodies, these warnings became a pop culture icon, transcending the walls of courtrooms.

As time passed, Miranda warnings faced their own share of courtroom drama. Lawyers argued over the timing of the warning, the mental state of suspects, and adaptations for minors or those with limited English proficiency.

Since 1966, the legal landscape has never been the same. From the silent era of self-incrimination to the age of constitutional safeguards, it's a tale of evolution, challenges, and rights that echo loudly. As the legal script continues to unfold, one thing remains crystal clear: the Miranda warning, once an unassuming line in a courtroom, has become a legal legend for the ages.

In the silence of justice, Miranda rights speak loudly, ensuring that even in custody, the accused are heard.

Notable Cases

Sometimes, crime and punishment transcend the courtroom, morphing into cultural landmarks that rival the suspense of blockbuster movies. These tales spark debates at dinner parties and compel you to double-check your locks at night. So, grab your popcorn as we journey into the notorious criminal cases that left an indelible mark on the landscape of law enforcement.

Let's kick things off with the granddaddy of them all—the O.J. Simpson trial in 1995. The former NFL star was accused of a brutal double murder, a high-stakes trial broadcasted live, and those infamous gloves that refused to cooperate. It's a true crime drama that riveted the nation, earning its title as the "Trial of the Century," as if other centuries were mere dress rehearsals.

Then there's the bone-chilling narrative of Ted Bundy, whose crimes spanned from the 1970s. Bundy, the charismatic serial killer, elevated manipulation to an art form. Envision a world where a seemingly affable man could be a heartless murderer, ensnaring victims with charm. Bundy's case showcased the significance of forensic evidence and the sobering fact that evil can masquerade as charm.

No discussion of iconic cases would be complete without the Manson Family murders—a tale of a magnetic cult leader orchestrating gruesome slayings that sent shock waves through Hollywood and the entire nation during the late 1960s and early 1970s. It's a horror movie made real, where the line between reality and fiction blurs, and law enforcement grapples with dismantling a cult's reign of terror.

Zooming ahead to the contemporary scene, the saga of Casey Anthony emerged in 2011—a young mother accused of killing her two-year-old daughter. The trial became a media frenzy, ensnaring audiences with twists and turns. It's a perplexing puzzle where the pieces don't quite fit, leaving everyone scratching their heads and dissecting the verdict.

And then there's the enigmatic tale of the Unabomber, Ted Kaczynski—an intellectual recluse who sent explosive parcels through the mail as his twisted protest against technology. Between 1978 and 1995, Kaczynski's reign of terror targeted those he deemed responsible for the erosion of nature and freedom. Though the very concept of a "lone wolf" was embodied, reminding us that malevolent genius can reside in unexpected packages.

But these cases aren't mere sensationalism; they've profoundly impacted law enforcement practices. The O.J. Simpson trial unveiled the media's influence and the challenge of upholding a fair trial in the public gaze. Bundy's case redefined forensic evidence and the art of profiling serial killers. The Manson Family murders compelled law enforcement to comprehend and counter the potency of cults. Casey Anthony's trial underscored the complexities of child homicide cases and the significance of constructing a compelling narrative in court. Lastly, the Unabomber case spotlighted the prowess of forensic linguistics in identifying and apprehending criminals.

Sifting through these gripping cases, a singular truth becomes evident: they transcend the domain of criminal narratives to shape how law enforcement navigates investigations, trials, and justice. From courtroom theatrics to the chilling details of the crimes, these captivating cases stand as enduring reminders that the world of law and order mirrors any Hollywood masterpiece's intrigue, excitement, and complexity.

Notable cases illuminate the complexities of our justice system, reminding us that truth often hides in the shadows.

Criminal Profiling

The Sherlock Holmes of the law enforcement world. Exploring the murky depths of criminal minds, this psychological tool has been fascinating and eyebrow-raising. Imagine if detectives could just sprinkle some psychological fairy dust and unveil a criminal's inner workings. While not quite magic, it has left its mark on the world of crime-solving.

The voyage of criminal profiling starts with the iconic case of Jack the Ripper, way back in the late 1800s. Authorities scratched their heads as the infamous serial killer left a trail of mutilated bodies in Victorian London. Then came Dr. Thomas Bond, a pathologist who dared to peek into the abyss of Jack's mind. He drafted a profile attempting to unmask the Ripper's age, habits, and occupation.

Moving into the 20th century, and the birth of the FBI's Behavioral Science Unit in the 1970s. These modern-day sleuths, led by John Douglas and Robert Ressler, sharpened the art of criminal profiling with their work on infamous cases like the "Co-Ed Killer" Edmund Kemper and the "Son of Sam" David Berkowitz. They set the stage for profiling to become the rock star of investigative tools.

As profiling evolved, its big moment came with the hunt for the Unabomber, Ted Kaczynski, in the 1990s. Meet James Fitzgerald, a linguist who entered the scene with his analysis of the Unabomber's manifesto. This wasn't just any vocabulary dissection; it was a textual showdown. The team's linguistic profile eventually led to Kaczynski's capture, proving that a criminal's words can be a window into their mind.

And what about the infamous "Mad Bomber" of New York, George Metesky, in the mid-1900s? James Brussel, who conjured an eerily on-point profile. He envisioned a homebody with a liking for precision and a possible obsession with Con Edison. The police nabbed Metesky, and voila! The power of profiling emerged from the shadows.

But profiling isn't all rainbows and breakthroughs. The Atlanta child murders in the late 1970s and early 1980s. Racial tension bubbled as a predominantly African-American community was plagued by child abductions and murders. The FBI's profile leaned heavily on a single offender. Still, history raised its eyebrows as doubts emerged about the accuracy of the profile. Two men were eventually convicted, but the case leaves us pondering the fine line between science and presumption.

As technology evolved, so did profiling. In the digital age, cybercriminals took center stage, creating cyber profiling – think of it as catching criminals in the web of their digital breadcrumbs. Experts analyze online behavior, pounce on digital footprints, and unravel the tangled web of ones and zeroes to catch modern-day crooks.

Criminal profiling, with its moments of brilliance and missteps, continues to weave its way through the fabric of crime-solving. From the days of Jack the Ripper to the digital age of cyber profiling, it's an expedition filled with intrigue and the occasional eyebrow-raising prediction. As law enforcement evolves, so does the quest to understand the enigmatic minds on the other side of the law.

In the art of criminal profiling, investigators decode the human mind, unraveling the mysteries of motive and method.

Cold Cases

The world of cold cases – where mysteries linger like forgotten leftovers in the back of the fridge. These enigmatic tales of unsolved crimes have haunted detectives and armchair sleuths alike, leaving us all scratching our heads and muttering, "Who dunnit?"

We start with the 1947 Black Dahlia murder – a Hollywood nightmare that has left everyone from gumshoe detectives to conspiracy theorists in a tizzy. Elizabeth Short's gruesome murder remains unsolved, shrouding her story in a dark cloud of mystery.

Skip ahead a few years to the 1950s and the Chicago Lipstick Murders – a case that left a trail of lipstick-stained notes and confusion. Yes, someone was leaving cryptic messages in lipstick. It's like a noir film gone wild, complete with a dash of glam.

After that, of course, there's the infamous case of the Zodiac Killer in the late 1960s and early 1970s. This elusive criminal taunted the police and media with cryptic letters and ciphers. Imagine a villain straight out of a comic book with a menacing costume and a penchant for riddles. This cold case has kept amateur sleuths glued to their magnifying glasses, trying to crack the Zodiac's code.

Then, DNA technology brought new life into old cases. The 1984 murder of Jonelle Matthews, a 12-year-old Colorado girl, went cold for decades until her remains were discovered in 2019. Advances in DNA analysis led to the arrest of a suspect, showing that even the coldest of cases can thaw under the heat of scientific progress.

Not all cold cases are solved with a triumphant "gotcha!" In fact, many remain stubbornly unsolved, like the case of the "Boy in the Box" from 1957. This unidentified child's body was found in a cardboard box in Pennsylvania, launching one of the most haunting cold cases in history. It's comparable to a real-life mystery novel, leaving readers clamoring for answers that may never come.

While some cold cases may remain forever frigid, others find closure in the most unexpected ways. Advances in forensics and technology continue to thaw out mysteries that have chilled us to the bone for decades. DNA matches, fingerprints, and old-fashioned persistence are like warm blankets in the icy world of unsolved crime.

Cold cases remind us that some mysteries, whether the Black Dahlia, the Zodiac Killer, or the Boy in the Box, are too stubborn to be forgotten. They challenge our wits, tease our curiosity, and keep us flipping through the pages of history in search of those elusive answers.

Cold cases are the ghosts of the past, but in the pursuit of justice, they are never forgotten.

Police Gadgets

The history of police "tools." When billy clubs and whistles were the peak of law enforcement innovation. The good ol' days when a stern talking-to and a swing of a club were all it took to keep the peace.

Turning back the clock to the 1800s, when the trusty billy club debuted – a timeless classic that says, "Behave or prepare to feel the thud." Then, in the 1880s, behold, the police whistle. This ear-piercing marvel can summon help or double as a canine concert conductor.

With the 20th century here, the portable tear gas dispenser arrived. Nothing says "let's clear the room" like a cloud of eye-watering, nose-tickling gas. By the 1970s, the first bulletproof vest entered the scene of law enforcement, turning officers into walking armadillos. Similar to strapping on a medieval suit of armor but with a modern twist.

The 1970s brought the iconic and nifty PR-24 side-handle baton – a law enforcement Swiss Army knife. And just when you thought things couldn't get any more interesting, the Taser also stuns its way into action in the 1970s, proving that zapping miscreants with electricity is the new norm. It resembles a high-voltage game of tag, and the Taser is "it."

As we venture further, the 1980s usher in the era of pepper spray, the spicy alternative to clubbing that brings a whole new meaning to "feeling the burn." By the 1990s, the world of crime-fighting was in the digital age, with officers chatting away on police radios like 90s teenagers on corded landline phones. But behold, the 21st century arrived with a bang – introducing body cameras in 2005. Now, every police interaction is recorded, making cops both crime fighters and instant movie stars.

Then, the rise of advanced forensics, from the fingerprinting marvels of the early 20th century to the DNA profiling breakthroughs of the late 20th century. Because nothing says "we've got your number," like irrefutable evidence that can't be argued with.

A riveting stroll through the history of "police tools," from the swinging billy club to the shocking Taser, from the deafening whistle to the sizzling pepper spray. It's a saga of innovation, a symphony of security, and a tale of tools that have evolved alongside the ever-changing landscape of law enforcement.

In the arsenal of technology, gadgets are the instruments of law enforcement, turning the impossible into the possible.

Serial Killers

Hold onto your sanity as we step into the dark corners of a serial killer's mind and explore the heinous crimes, bizarre motives, and the haunting specter of law enforcement's relentless pursuit. A journey that will make your skin crawl and remind you that reality can be more horrifying than any work of fiction.

Beginning with the one and only Jack the Ripper, a mysterious figure who terrorized the Whitechapel district of London in the late 1800s. A gloomy fog-filled backdrop, shadowy alleyways, and the grisly murders of at least five women. A Gothic novel comes to life, complete with a sinister twist. Jack's favorite pastime? Disemboweling his victims with surgical precision. Oh, how quaint! And the best part? Despite a flurry of theories and suspects, this villain vanished into thin air, leaving detectives scratching their heads and history buffs pondering over tea.

Moving to the 1970s, meet the Son of Sam, aka David Berkowitz, a real charmer who prowled the streets of New York City. This guy wasn't content with just one title – he wanted to keep the whole city on edge. With a gun in hand and a thirst for blood, Berkowitz shot and killed six people and wounded several others.

His weapon of choice? A .44 caliber revolver, which he dubbed his "equalizer" because apparently, he needed an "equal" to compete with innocent lives. Berkowitz claimed he was taking orders from a demon-possessed dog. Yes, evidently, this dog had some profound influence over him. Maybe we should've started a pet therapy program for criminals.

Last but certainly not least, we have the "Killer Clown" himself, John Wayne Gacy, who managed to combine two of humanity's greatest fears – clowns and serial killers. Gacy's twisted antics occurred between 1972 and 1978 when kids' parties and death were not usually mentioned in the same sentence.

This delightful fellow would dress up as "Pogo the Clown" and entertain children at events, all while secretly burying bodies in the crawl space of his home. Talk about multitasking! In total, Gacy murdered 33 young men, proving that sometimes the monsters really are hiding behind the laughter.

These "people" shed light on the dark corners of the human psyche, the frailty of the human mind, and the painstaking efforts of law enforcement to catch these elusive villains.

In the darkness of the human soul, serial killers are the monsters we fear, but law enforcement is the light that protects us.

Forensic Science

In the world of crime-solving, forensic science takes center stage. This real-life magic turns crime scenes into laboratories, where evidence speaks volumes and mysteries unravel in a puff of logic. Every piece of evidence tells a story – almost like a theatrical episode of CSI.

The crime scene with clues scattered like confetti, and then enters the DNA analysis – the superhero of forensic science. A genetic detective sifting through the microscopic bits to unveil the perpetrator's identity. Who knew that the blueprint of life would be the ultimate crime-fighting tool?

The O.G. of forensic evidence: fingerprints. It resembles your personal seal of identification, left behind on every surface you touch. And the forensic experts? They're like fingerprint whisperers, decoding the whorls and ridges to catch criminals red-handed – or should we say, fingerprinted.

Then there's ballistics – the science of matching bullets to guns, a bit like a bullet's tell-all diary. Firearms experts study the unique markings that bullets and casings leave on fired rounds, creating a ballistic fingerprint. It's reminiscent of connecting the dots. Only the dots are made of gunpowder and lead.

But forensic science isn't limited to fingerprints and bullet trajec-tories; it's a treasure trove of techniques that sound like something out of a sci-fi movie. Bite mark analysis? Yep, that's a thing – like dental impressions for criminal teeth. Footprint analysis? Absolutely – because even shoes can tell a story. Hair and fiber analysis? Of course – because even the most minor strand can be a clue.

The kingpin of the whole crime lab – the DNA database. Similar to a massive genetic Rolodex where every cheek swab and crime scene sample can be cross-referenced, revealing previously invisible links. Like every cell carries a silent witness to the crime.

When exploring the riveting world of forensic science, one thing becomes clear: it's more than just test tubes and microscopes; it's the art of transforming evidence into narratives, of revealing hidden stories in bloodstains and fibers. From DNA analysis to fingerprinting and the intriguing science of ballistics, forensic science is a symphony of science and deduction that unravels mysteries one piece of evidence at a time.

In the microscopic world of evidence, forensic science unveils the truth, speaking for the voiceless and the fallen.

IV

Firefighting Follies

Welcome, dear reader, to a realm where bravery meets hilarity, where heroes charge into blazing infernos while occasionally pondering which end of the hose to point where. In 'Firefighting Follies,' we delve into the boisterous history of those intrepid souls who've battled flames, complete with Dalmatians who appeared to be the real brains behind the operation and firefighters who slid down poles with more flair than a Broadway diva taking her final bow.

Bucket Brigades

A h, gather 'round, for we're about to embark on a journey to the days when firefighting was less about sleek fire engines and more about passing the torch – or rather, the bucket. Yes, you heard that right, a bucket. A bustling colonial town where the menace of fire lurked like a mischievous rascal waiting for the right moment to turn buildings into infernos. Enter the heroes of yore, the champions of community resilience – the bucket brigades!

Back in the 1700s, these brave souls were the first line of defense against fiery chaos. When an alarm sounded, people from all walks of life dropped their quills, put down their mutton chops, and rallied to form human chains. Each link in the chain clutched a leather bucket filled with water, which they passed with utmost urgency. It was like a real-life game of "hot potato," but it was a sizzling situation that needed dousing instead of a spud.

Now, let's talk about those leather buckets. These weren't your run-of-the-mill pails; oh no, these were symbols of safety woven with communal pride. Families engraved their names on these buckets and displayed them with seriousness and flair, like a vintage Instagram post saying, "We're ready to tackle fire – are you?" These buckets were like membership cards to an exclusive firefighting club. This membership came with the right to hoist and pass with gusto.

And let's recognize the unsung heroes of these bucket brigades: the bucket makers. These skilled artisans were what Michelin-star chefs are, from leather buckets to gourmet dining. They meticulously crafted functional buckets showcasing a bit of local flavor. Some even had intricate designs and craftsmanship that spoke volumes about the community's dedication to fire safety.

When you hear the wailing sirens of a modern fire engine, take a moment to tip your imaginary tricorn hat to the bucket brigades of yore. They may not have had water cannons or thermal imaging cameras, but they had something even more powerful – a shared purpose and a commitment to protecting their community one bucket at a time.

In unity, we form a chain stronger than any fire, passing buckets of hope to douse the flames of despair.

Turnout Gear

Beneath the billowing smoke and amidst the towering infernos, the brave souls of the firefighting world have battled blazes with more than just courage—they've been equipped with an evolving fashion show of turnout gear that combines functionality, protection and a dash of that unmistakable firefighter flair.

Back in the good ol' days of yore, firefighters suited up in whatever they could scrounge up: maybe an old coat, some leather gloves, and a hearty dose of "let's hope for the best." It was a wild blend of improvisation and desperation that probably had the flames laughing more than quaking in fear.

Then came the 19th century, a time of enlightenment and invention, where folks realized that maybe, just maybe, wearing woolen garments soaked in water wasn't the best strategy for dealing with fires. Thus, the first attempts at organized firefighting attire emerged: long coats, leather helmets, and something akin to crude rain gear. It was less "flame-resistant" and more "let's hope this doesn't melt."

Fast-forward to the 20th century, when firefighters got a techno-logical makeover. Infamous asbestos. Turns out, asbestos was like the superhero fabric of the time—it could withstand heat like a champ. Unfortunately, it also had a nasty habit of releasing toxic fibers into the air. But hey, who needs lung health when you've got flame-resistant capabilities?

Thankfully, science soon saved the day by introducing modern materials like Nomex and Kevlar. These fancy fabrics offered firefighters actual protection without the side dish of lung problems. Suits got sleeker, helmets got tougher, and firefighters collectively breathed a sigh of relief—literally.

Then came the 21st century, where innovation became the name of the game. Firefighting gear started looking more like spacesuits, complete with built-in communication systems, thermal imaging cameras, and, who knows, maybe even a built-in espresso machine for those long nights at the station.

Then there's the evolution of visibility. Gone are the days of "blend into the smoke and hope for the best." Today's firefighters strut their stuff in high-visibility and reflective strips that practically scream, "Hey, look at me! I'm here to save the day and look fabulous doing it!"

And it's not just about looking good; it's about staying cool. Literally, modern turnout gear incorporates moisture-wicking fabrics, ventilation systems, and layers upon layers of high-tech materials designed to keep firefighters from spontaneously combusting inside their suits.

There you have it: the sartorial evolution of firefighting turnout gear, from woolen coats to high-tech ensembles that make you wonder if firefighters are secretly preparing for an intergalactic firefighting contest. While the aesthetics may have changed, one thing remains constant: the unwavering dedication of those who don the gear and charge into danger, looking as fierce as they do functional. So here's to the firefighters, the real-life superheroes who have traded in their capes for flame-resistant capes, ready to battle the flames while keeping their fashion-forward sensibilities intact.

Clad in armor of valor, firefighters face the inferno, their turnout gear a shield against the fury of flames.

Fire Hydrants

The unsung heroes of the urban landscape: fire hydrants. These trusty sentinels stand proudly along sidewalks, ready to burst into action with a splash of water at a moment's notice. But where did these life-saving water fountains come from, and how did they become the icon of emergency response that they are today? Prepare yourself for a history lesson that's wetter than a rainy day in a water park.

Our story begins in the early 19th century when fires were extinguished by a ragtag crew wielding leather buckets and the sheer force of desperation. It wasn't a pretty sight, but it was all they had. Then came along a clever inventor named George Smith, who decided to give firefighters a fighting chance. In 1817, Smith patented the first fire hydrant—a wooden contraption with a valve that could regulate water flow. It was like a plumbing miracle, and Smith became the unsung hero of soggy heroes everywhere.

But wait, there's more! Skip ahead to 1869, when a fellow named Frederick Graff Sr. took things to the next level. He crafted the "Philadelphia Model," which featured an underground water main connected to a hydrant above ground. No more lugging buckets or praying for rain; now firefighters had a direct line to water like a superhero with a utility belt full of hydration.

Of course, it wouldn't be a historical story without a dash of drama.

Different cities had their own ideas about hydrant designs, leading to a chaotic mix of shapes and sizes. It was like a hydrant beauty pageant gone horribly wrong—tall hydrants, short hydrants, chubby hydrants, you name it.

Thankfully, a hero emerged from this hydrant chaos: Birdseye Frost, an engineer who introduced the "Frost Free Hydrant" in 1874. This innovative design prevented freezing, which was a game-changer for cold climates. Suddenly, firefighters didn't have to wrestle with frozen hydrants like they were trying to tame a frosty beast.

As time marched on, hydrants got even more sophisticated. In the 20th century, dry barrel hydrants were invented, which prevented water from freezing in the underground pipe. And the introduction of color-coded caps that signaled the water pressure available—a veritable rainbow of water readiness.

Nowadays, fire hydrants are as ubiquitous as squirrels in a park. They come in various shapes and sizes, some even dressed up in fancy artistic designs to beautify city streets. But beneath the aesthetics lies the same spirit of heroism that has saved countless homes, businesses, and maybe even a cat or two.

So, there you have it, the riveting history of fire hydrants—a tale of innovation, freezing struggles, and a quest for the perfect way to deliver water on demand.

In the quiet streets, they stand sentinel, ready to unleash the life-giving flow that quells the fiery tempest.

Fire Mark Plaques

Transport yourself to a time when fire insurance wasn't just a policy but a visual spectacle adorning the facades of buildings. Yes, you've entered the world of the 18th and 19th centuries, where fire mark insurance plaques weren't just about coverage; they were about displaying fire safety in style. Imagine a cobblestone street lined with buildings, each with a unique badge that screamed, "I'm insured, and I'm proud of it!"

In those days, insurance wasn't just a contract but a proclamation of responsibility. Fire insurance companies of the past understood the power of symbolism, which led to creating fire mark plaques. These plaques, made from durable materials like cast iron or copper, showcased the company's emblem, serving as a double-edged sword of information and reassurance. It's as if the buildings became spokespersons, telling tales of preparedness through these badges of honor.

But let's not reduce these plaques to mere marketing tools. They were symbols of a burgeoning firefighting ethos, an acknowledgment that amidst the roaring flames, some structures were fortified against disaster. Think of a brave firefighter rushing to a blaze, spotting the distinctive emblem, and realizing that not all heroes wear capes – some wear fire mark plaques. Saving these buildings wasn't just about protecting property but honoring a commitment to fire safety in an era where extinguishing flames was a mix of science and sorcery.

As we stroll through the digital age with insurance policies accessible at our fingertips, it's easy to appreciate the tangible nature of fire mark plaques. They were more than just metal; they embodied a promise, a physical reminder that responsibility was displayed for all to see. These plaques adorned townhouses and shops, silently announcing that their owners took fire safety seriously. In a time when fire engines were still horse-drawn and firefighters wore leather helmets, these plaques bridged the gap between old-world aesthetics and modern-day sensibilities.

When you glance at a modern insurance advertisement or ponder the intricacies of property protection, take a moment to tip your metaphorical hat to those pioneers of property assurance. Those fire mark plaques weren't just decorative; they were statements of security, forging a link between past and present in a way that only history can.

Marked by courage, our plaques tell the story of those who protect and serve, a testament to bravery etched in metal.

Firefighting Tools

From ancient blunders to modern marvels, the evolution of firefighting tools is a tale as old as...well, fire.

Back in the day—way back—our caveman ancestors probably used, I don't know, wet leaves and mammoth bones to combat fires. Not the most effective strategy, but hey, it was a start. Moving on to ancient civilizations, and you've got bucket brigades passing water in a comically ineffective human chain. Nothing says "organized disaster" like a line of people drenching each other more than the actual fire.

But fear not, for innovation eventually kicked in. The Romans, for instance, introduced a nifty tool called the "siphon." It was basically a water pump powered by—you guessed it—people. Sure, it required a bit of manual labor, but it was better than relying on a neighboring village's bucket.

The Middle Ages brought about a fire-igniting frenzy (not the good kind). In came the "fire hook," a long pole with a hook on the end to pull down burning buildings. Because, you know, grappling with flames from a safe distance seemed like a logical plan.

Leaping into the Renaissance, where things got a tad more creative. Fire engines with hand-operated pumps were developed. They looked like horse-drawn torture devices, but hey, they could actually spray water! And let's not forget the leather fire buckets that doubled as status symbols—you weren't anybody unless you had a bucket with your name on it.

The 19th century saw the birth of the steam fire engine. This contraption looked like a cross between a locomotive and a metal octopus. It could pump water and propel itself, a true marvel of machinery that probably terrified more horses than it saved buildings.

As time marched on, firefighters needed better ways to communicate. Enter the "gamewell box," a pull-alarm system that turned firefighters into unwitting participants in the world's most intense game of tug-of-war. Pulling the lever activated a bell, alerting the fire station and every dog within a ten-mile radius.

Then came the motorized era, with motorized fire trucks replacing horse-drawn carriages. It was like upgrading from a bicycle to a rocket ship. And don't forget the invention of the smoke mask, which allowed firefighters to enter burning buildings without choking on their own bravery.

Today, firefighting tools are a blend of high-tech wizardry and old-school practicality. We have thermal imaging cameras that make seeing through smoke look like a superhero's party trick. And the "jaws of life," hydraulic tools that can rip apart cars like a kid tearing open a Christmas present.

Firefighting tools have come a long way, from siphons to smoke masks. And while we've left the days of water-pulling human chains behind, the spirit of fighting fires remains as fierce as ever.

Tools of the trade, each one a trusted companion, empowering firefighters to conquer adversity and protect their communities.

Fire Poles

L adies and gentlemen, gather 'round the proverbial firehouse hearth as we plunge into the captivating history of fire poles – those iconic elements that save precious seconds and ignite a sense of nostalgia in the hearts of firefighting aficionados. Visualize yourself in the vibrant 1870s, where roaring fires still held sway, and firefighting was more of an art than a science. In this era, a brilliant and pragmatic Detroit firefighter named David Kenyon set out to revolutionize how firefighters descended from their towering perches.

Detroit, Michigan – a city known for its automobile legacy and, as it turns out, its contribution to firefighting innovation. David Kenyon, a firefighter in the Motor City, recognized that time was of the essence when it came to dashing from the upper floors of fire stations to the ground floor where the fire engines awaited. Stairs simply weren't efficient enough; they were too slow for the rapid response that battling fires demanded.

And so, like a knight in turnout gear, Kenyon rode to the rescue with a brilliant idea – the fire pole. An ingenious solution inspired by the world of quick thinking and action, the fire pole allowed firefighters to slide down from the upper floors to the ground floor at breakneck speed. They no longer had to wrestle with stairs or worry about being fashionably late to a blazing spectacle. With the fire pole, they could make a stylish and lightning-fast entrance, which we imagine felt something like an early version of a superhero swooping down to save the day.

Picture, if you will, the camaraderie among firefighters as they lined up in formation, ready to descend in what must have seemed like an adrenaline-fueled ballet of gravity. The clatter of boots, the whir of turnout gear, and the echoes of cheers created a symphony of teamwork and determination. It was more than just a practical solution; it was a statement – a declaration that firefighters were not just ordinary citizens but a league of extraordinary individuals united in their mission to safeguard lives and property.

While reflecting on this inventive marvel, let's also tip our helmets to the firefighters of yesteryears. Their courage was matched only by their ingenuity, and their legacy lives on in the modern firehouses that still embrace the swift descent of the fire pole. While we may have entered the era of high-tech equipment and sleek fire engines, the fire pole has a certain charm that reminds us of the unbreakable bond between firefighting history and the heroes shaping it.

In the future, if you encounter a fire pole – whether in a historic fire station or on the silver screen – take a moment to salute the visionary spirit of David Kenyon and the countless firefighters who have followed in his daring footsteps. With a touch of levity and a whole lot of courage, they slid their way into firefighting lore, leaving an indelible mark on the very essence of rapid response.

Thus, the journey through the world of fire poles concludes, leaving us with a newfound appreciation for the art of firefighting and the whimsical yet practical solutions that have shaped its evolution. Heroes don't always wear capes; sometimes, they slide down poles with a grin, ready to take on whatever the flames throw their way.

Descending into the heart of danger, firefighters slide down poles of purpose, answering the call with unwavering resolve.

Firefighter Training

Hold onto your fire helmets because we're diving headfirst into the sizzling history of firefighting training. Yes, that's right, folks. Before those brave souls could confidently charge into the fiery abyss, they had to figure out which end of the hose spouted water.

Back in ancient times, training was more like a baptism by fire. Picture a group of well-meaning villagers staring at a raging inferno and thinking, "I guess we should do something about that." This was the golden era of "winging it," where heroics and chaos danced the macarena side by side.

The Middle Ages brought us the "bucket brigade drill," where firefighters would simulate a fire by passing empty buckets around, giggling, and pretending that buckets contained mystical flames. Genius, right? Nothing hones your firefighting skills quite like a vigorous game of pass-the-imaginary-bucket.

Jumping to the Renaissance, and we witness the birth of "the bucket brigade with actual water." Revolutionary, I know. This high-stakes exercise involved dousing a fire with actual water, proving that firefighters had finally figured out which end of the bucket was up.

The 18th century saw the advent of "fire pole sliding," as firefighters realized that descending from elevated surfaces needed an element of style. It was basically the original firefighter Olympics, with bonus points awarded for not landing on your fellow comrades.

As the 19th century rolled around, a more structured approach emerged. Firefighting academies popped up, probably because they finally realized that the "trial by fire" technique had a significant downside. Recruits were subjected to a rigorous regimen of bucket-lugging, ladder-climbing, and shouted orders, leaving everyone feeling like they were in a never-ending game of firefighter Simon Says.

The 20th century brought a bit of modernity to the scene. Firefighters were now being taught how to use actual fire hoses, which was a game-changer considering their previous experiences with imaginary buckets. And don't forget the trusty "stop, drop, and roll" maneuver for extinguishing personal flames. Because every firefighter secretly aspires to be a human burrito.

Today, firefighting training is a well-oiled machine of education and preparation. Recruits learn everything from life-saving techniques to advanced tactics for tackling towering infernos. They're also taught how to rescue cats from trees because the world simply can't get enough of that heartwarming cliché.

From the days of "let's hope we don't die" to the modern era of "let's hope we don't die, but with actual knowledge," firefighting training has come a long way. If you see a firefighter in action, recognize that behind those fierce flames and heroic poses lies a history of flailing bucket brigades and firefighters sliding down poles like dashing daredevils.

Through sweat and sacrifice, we forge heroes in the crucible of training, preparing them to face the hottest of challenges.

Dalmatians

I n firefighting lore, where towering flames meet fearless heroes, a rather unexpected character emerges – the spotted and energetic Dalmatian. Those elegant dogs that often grace firehouse posters and children's books aren't just there for show; they have a storied history intertwined with the art of firefighting itself.

It's the 19th century, a time when horse-drawn fire carriages were as typical as blacksmiths and cobblestone streets. As firefighters rushed to the scene of a blaze, their trusty steeds carried them with urgency and purpose. But there was a challenge – horses, like humans, could become anxious in the chaos of an emergency. That's where Dalmatians came into play. They could connect with horses and calm them amid the raging storm.

Envision a Dalmatian perched atop a horse-drawn fire carriage, its distinctive spots standing out against the backdrop of smoke and urgency. These canine travelers were more than just fellow travelers; they were the calming influence that turned wary horses into staunch collaborators in combating fires. Their calming influence was more than a quirk; it was a practical solution that kept both firefighters and their noble steeds safe during the high-stakes missions to quell roaring blazes.

The question is, why Dalmatians? Their history included roles as carriage dogs and guardians, making them natural choices to accompany firefighters on their expeditions. Dalmatians immediately established themselves as dependable companions, forging a special connection that united the animal and human worlds thanks to their propensity for running alongside horses.

Fast forward to the present, and Dalmatians are still revered symbols of firefighting heritage. Their presence in firehouses and parades is a nod to their historical significance and a celebration of their unique ability to form connections – whether with horses or the human heart. As mascots and living symbols of the relationship between the past and present, these spotted sidekicks have earned their position in the pantheon of firefighters.

If you get the opportunity to see a Dalmatian perched proudly next to a firefighter, remember that their history goes beyond aesthetics. They are the unsung heroes who once calmed the chaos, turning frenzied scenes into moments of harmony and cooperation. They're the four-legged legends whose spots aren't just patterns but imprints of a legacy that continues to blaze on.

A Dalmatian's spots may be black and white, but their loyalty to firefighters is painted in the colors of devotion.

Chicago Fire of 1871

Prepare to travel back to a fateful day that etched its fiery mark on history – the Great Chicago Fire of 1871. Visualize the sprawling metropolis of Chicago, a city on the cusp of greatness, suddenly plunged into chaos as flames danced and buildings crumbled. While learning about this tragic but transformative event, let's explore how the fire sparked destruction and a renewed spirit of resilience and rebuilding.

In the annals of urban legends, the story of the Great Chicago Fire occupies a prominent chapter. The fire's origin is often attributed to the O'Leary family's cow kicking over a lantern, igniting a barn, and setting the city ablaze. While this tale has been debated over the years, what remains undisputed is the scale of the catastrophe. The fire raged through the city for two days, consuming nearly 3.3 square miles of land, destroying 17,400 buildings, and leaving a trail of destruction in its wake.

But here's where the tale takes an unexpected turn – the fire's aftermath wasn't despair but determination. Chicagoans faced adversity head-on, refusing to be defined by the destruction. As the embers cooled and the smoke cleared, the city's leaders and residents rallied together, determined to rebuild Chicago stronger and safer than ever before.

The fire's impact extended beyond Chicago's borders, capturing the nation's attention and sparking conversations about fire safety, urban planning, and disaster preparedness. This tragic event ignited a movement for change, leading to improvements in building codes, fire prevention measures, and firefighting techniques. The fire itself became a catalyst for progress, a reminder that even in the face of devastation, humanity can find the strength to rise from the ashes.

Think about this scene: a cityscape transformed, with modern buildings replacing the charred remnants of the past. Architects and planners designed structures prioritizing fire resistance, and communities adopted new strategies to prevent future catastrophes. The Great Chicago Fire of 1871 had taught a powerful lesson – that from destruction emerges the opportunity for rebirth, a concept that resonates through history.

While we reflect on this pivotal moment, think back to the devastation and the indomitable spirit that emerged from the ashes. The Great Chicago Fire of 1871 wasn't just a blaze; it was a turning point that united a city and a nation in the face of adversity. It stands as a testament to human resolve, a reminder that even the darkest moments can illuminate the path toward progress.

The next time you stroll through Chicago's bustling streets or glimpse a skyline touched by modern architecture, recollect on the fire that transformed the city's trajectory. It's a reminder that amid the ruins of tragedy, hope can sprout like a phoenix, soaring to new heights.

Take a moment to honor the memory of those who endured this trial by fire by celebrating their resilience and the enduring legacy of rebuilding that defines Chicago and cities worldwide. May we always remember that while flames may scorch, they also have the power to forge a prominent, brighter future.

From the ashes of tragedy rose the phoenix of resilience, as Chicago rebuilt itself with the indomitable spirit of its people.

Brotherhood and Sisterhood

Get ready to unlock the secrets of the firefighting brotherhood and sisterhood, where camaraderie and unity are as hot as a five-alarm blaze. Yes, folks, even hotter than those well-worn fire boots you've seen kicking around.

Flashback to ancient times, when humans discovered that working together could be pretty handy, especially when your village was under siege by the dreaded "unwanted fire guest." Imagine a ragtag group of brave souls armed with buckets of water, glaring at the flames with determination. And voila! The seeds of the firefighting brotherhood were planted, watered, and doused in glorious unity.

Fast forward to medieval Europe, where the concept of "mutual aid societies" began to take shape. These were like the original "I've got your back" clubs, where local townsfolk would band together to save their thatched-roofed homes from fiery devastation. It was essentially a medieval potluck, where everyone brought their buckets and bravery.

By the 19th century, firefighting had become a well-oiled machine of teamwork. Fire companies, often run by volunteers, would race to the scene, each determined to be the first to extinguish the flames and earn bragging rights for the next century. It was like a high-stakes game of "who can be the most heroic while wearing suspenders."

And then came the dawn of the 20th century, when firefighting became a full-fledged profession. Firefighters began to see themselves not just as individuals battling blazes but as a brotherhood (and eventually a sisterhood, too) united by the common goal of saving lives and property. Firehouses became second homes, and colleagues became family members who knew way too much about each other's quirks and favorite late-night snacks.

The sense of camaraderie only grew stronger with time. Firefighters started using lingo that only their fellow brethren and sistren could understand. "Size up" wasn't about their morning coffee; "rollover" wasn't about turning in bed; and "staging area" wasn't about a spot to practice your jazz hands routine. But hey, every exclusive club needs its secret handshake, right?

Today, the firefighting brotherhood and sisterhood is stronger than ever. Firefighters share a unique bond forged through shared challenges, countless drills, and enough inside jokes to fill a firehouse-sized book. They've got each other's backs, whether it's dousing flames, lifting spirits, or just finding the right channel on the firehouse TV.

When you see a group of firefighters giving each other that knowing nod or sharing a laugh during the chaos, remember that behind those helmets and bunker gear lies a history of unity, support, and a bond that can only be forged in the flames of friendship.

Bound not by blood, but by the shared oath, firefighters form a family, their solidarity unbreakable, their love unwavering.

V

Medical Mavericks

Prepare to don your metaphorical scrubs and step into the shoes of medical mavericks, those unsung heroes who wield stethoscopes like magic wands. In 'Medical Mavericks,' we'll explore the world of emergency medical services, where the iconic Star of Life shines brightly, paramedics make James Bond look like an amateur, and where every call is a life-or-death improv performance. Join us in a world where heroism and humor often share the same operating room.

The History of EMS

E mergency Medical Services (EMS) has come a long way from its humble beginnings, but don't expect smooth terrain. This adventure has its fair share of bumps, just like an ancient stretcher ride!

We kick things off in ancient Egypt around 2500 BC. The land of pyramids, pharaohs, and plagues. What did you get when you crossed paths with a snakebite or a spear in the wrong place? The world's first rudimentary stretcher – two sticks, some palm fronds, and a dash of hope. Not exactly an ambulance, but it did the trick. Then, in 460 BC, in Iconic Greek, we meet Hippocrates, the O.G. doctor. He gifted us with the Hippocratic Oath, the ancient version of "Thou shalt not play doctor without a license."

Now, let's spotlight ancient Rome, circa 500 AD. Gladiators in the Colosseum were all about high-stakes battles and low-tech medical care. When a gladiator found himself on the wrong end of a trident, out came the stretcher – two pieces of wood slapped together like a DIY project gone wrong. It wasn't a smooth ride, but it was better than being left for the lions.

The Renaissance brought us Ambroise Paré, a barber-surgeon who turned wound care into art. He reduced the agony of amputation and, in doing so, introduced a bit of finesse to pre-hospital care. Not bad for a guy who probably used the same tools for haircuts and amputations!

In the 18th century, Amsterdam debuted the first organized life-saving society for drowning victims. That's right, they had "societies" for drowning – and no, they didn't teach you how not to drown. Jumping ahead to the 19th century, Napoleon's chief surgeon, Dominique-Jean Larrey, rolled onto the scene with horse-drawn "ambulances volantes." They weren't exactly flying, but they did have horsepower.

The 20th century ushered in modern EMS, with motorized ambulances and World War I battlefield medicine improvements. Then, paramedics emerged as highly trained professionals with advanced life-saving gadgets. They were the superheroes of healthcare, minus the spandex suits (most of the time).

Today, EMS is a well-oiled machine, complete with paramedics, EMTs, ambulances that could probably time-travel, and a "Star of Life" symbol representing the six functions of EMS. It's a far cry from ancient Egypt's palm fronds and wooden planks.

In the chronicles of saving lives, the history of EMS is a testament to humanity's unwavering commitment to healing.

The Importance of the Star of Life

S peaking of the Star of Life, let's explore the meaning behind this iconic emblem. Designed by the National Highway Traffic Safety Administration (NHTSA) in the United States, this six-pointed star isn't just a symbol – it's a cosmic roadmap to the six essential functions of EMS.

It all began in the 1970s when the NHTSA, like a creative genius struck by lightning, decided that EMS needed a logo. But not just any logo – a logo that could encapsulate the very essence of pre-hospital care. Thus, the Star of Life was born in 1973, shining brighter than any disco ball at Studio 54.

Each of the six points of this celestial star represents a crucial function of EMS. Detection – because they can't save lives if they don't know there's an emergency happening. Reporting – seeing that, in the age of rotary phones, someone had to dial 911 and say, "Send help, quick!" Response – EMS responders don't leisurely saunter to emergencies; they race like they're auditioning for a NASCAR gig.

On-scene care – showing up isn't enough; they've got to do some medical magic right there on the spot. Care in transit – because it's not a party until you've got an ambulance as your chariot. And finally, transfer to definitive care – after the ambulance ride, you better believe there's more medical wizardry waiting at the hospital.

The Star of Life isn't just a cosmic trinket; it's a symbol of the relentless dedication of EMS professionals. They're the heroes who show up when disaster strikes, don their capes (metaphorically) and embark on a mission to save lives.

You might be wondering why a star? Why not a heart, a lightning bolt, or an ambulance with rocket boosters? Well, a star is timeless, like EMS itself. It shines through the darkness, guiding EMS responders to those in need, just like a beacon in the night.

The Star of Life shines as a symbol of hope, guiding EMS professionals through the darkest hours to deliver care and compassion.

The First Ambulance

We mentioned Napoleon's chief surgeon, Dominique-Jean Larrey, earlier. Let's jump into the story of the first-ever ambulance. Traveling back to the early 19th century, a time of epic battles and grand mustaches. In the Napoleonic Wars, where the term "roadside assistance" might as well have been in Latin, emerged Dominique-Jean Larrey, the genius behind the world's first recognized ambulance service.

Europe, the late 1700s. Armies clashed, muskets fired, and soldiers dropped like flies. But what happened when a soldier took an unexpected bayonet to the gut or a cannonball to the leg? Well, you could say it was a rough and tumble ride to medical care – emphasis on the tumble. The concept of battlefield medical transportation was as sophisticated as a unicycle in a Formula 1 race.

Then walked in Dominique-Jean Larrey, a French military surgeon with an eye for innovation. In 1797, while most people were still figuring out how to tie their shoelaces, Larrey proposed the idea of the "flying ambulance." No, it didn't have wings (that would be too fantastical), but it did have wheels – and lots of them. He envisioned a mobile medical unit that could swoop onto the battlefield like a superhero's chariot and whisk the wounded away to safety.

Larrey's ambitions didn't stop there. He is the mastermind behind the pièce de résistance: the horse-drawn ambulance. These weren't your everyday carriages; these were specially designed-vehicles with compartments to transport wounded soldiers lying down. The 19th-century version of a medical R.V., complete with bumpy roads and the occasional pothole.

Then, in 1810, Napoleon Bonaparte, that tiny general with grand plans, officially established the Ambulance de la Grande Armée. That's right, Napoleon himself gave the green light to Larrey's genius idea. He recognized the value of a well-oiled medical transport system, declaring, "An army cannot fight without provisions, and it cannot be furnished with them without the ambulance."

Larrey's ambulance service was a game-changer. It saved countless lives during the Napoleonic Wars, proving that a horse-drawn carriage could sometimes be mightier than a cannon. But let's not get too carried away; these early ambulances were hardly luxury vehicles. It was a bumpy, jolting ride on cobblestone streets, with wounded soldiers probably thinking, "I should've packed my Dramamine."

Today, when we think of ambulances, we envision high-tech vehicles with flashing lights, sirens, and paramedics ready to perform medical miracles. But it all started with Larrey's horse-drawn contraptions that were less "smooth ride" and more "wild horse chase."

With the first ambulance, we forged a path to those in need, a journey that continues to define the heart of EMS

The Evolution of EMS Vehicles

Fasten your seatbelts (or gurneys) as we embark on a whirlwind journey through time, tracing the evolution of EMS vehicles. From the clunky horse-drawn carriages of yesteryears to the high-tech, life-saving juggernauts we have today.

We've already mentioned 1797, a time when "ambulance" was synonymous with a rickety cart on four wheels. Dominique-Jean Larrey introduced the concept of the horse-drawn ambulance. These weren't your everyday carriages; they were more like wooden boxes on wheels, where wounded soldiers endured a roller coaster of pain on their way to medical care.

Jump ahead a few years to the 19th century. It wasn't all about horseplay. By the late 1800s, steam-powered ambulances chugged onto the scene. Imagine your local fire brigade rolling up to your doorstep in a miniature locomotive, ready to whisk you away to the hospital. Let's just say they were "steaming" ahead with innovation.

Fast forward to the early 20th century, and motorized ambulances made their grand entrance. These early motor vehicles had all the grace and style of a Model T Ford, but they got the job done. They were bulky and a bit unwieldy but revolutionary, like the first-generation smartphones of the ambulance world.

As the 20th century roared on, so did advancements in EMS vehicles. Fly-cars – those swanky sedans with essential medical equipment –

became favored for rapid response in urban areas. Picture a paramedic in a bowler hat and a stethoscope, dashing to the scene in a snazzy car like a medical Sherlock Holmes.

Now, modern ambulances are the true rockstars of EMS vehicles. These technologically advanced beasts come in various flavors, like the Type I ambulance, which is basically a mini-hospital on wheels, complete with all the bells and whistles of life support. Then there's the Type II ambulance, more like the family minivan of EMS, efficient but not as flashy. And last but not least, the Type III ambulance, a souped-up van that's ready to tackle medical mayhem.

But the real showstopper in the EMS vehicle lineup is the air medical service. Helicopters and planes swooping in like medical superheroes, airlifting patients to specialized care facilities. They're the Batmobiles of the EMS world, zipping through the skies to save the day. More on those coming up...

The evolution of EMS vehicles has been wild, from horse-drawn hurdles to high-tech heroes. We've gone from wooden boxes on wheels to mobile hospitals with all the gizmos and gadgets of modern medicine. It's not just a vehicle – it's a symbol of progress, innovation, and the unwavering commitment of EMS professionals to saving lives, one bumpy ride at a time.

From humble beginnings to modern marvels, EMS vehicles have raced against time to deliver aid where it's needed most.

Air Medical Services

Prepare to take flight as we soar through the history of air medical services, an industry that evolved from the pioneers of aviation and some seriously ambitious thinking.

It all began in the early 20th century when aviation was in its infancy. It was an era of biplanes, leather helmets, and the audacious belief that humans could conquer the skies. In 1928, a visionary named Lieutenant John A. Macready set the wheels in motion for air medical services when he used a biplane to transport a patient in critical condition. Yup, the first air ambulance was essentially a glorified crop duster with a patient in the backseat.

Twelve years later, in the 1940s, World War II was in full swing. The conflict provided a unique opportunity for medical aviation to take off, quite literally. The U.S. military deployed dedicated air evacuation units, often converting cargo planes into flying ambulances. It was the military version of "Extreme Makeover: Ambulance Edition," complete with stretchers and medical teams.

However, it wasn't until the late 1940s that civilian air medical services began gaining traction. Dr. James Styner, an orthopedic surgeon with a taste for adventure, helped establish the first civilian helicopter ambulance service in 1947. They aptly named it the "Flying Angels." Now, picture a doctor in a pilot's cap, flying a helicopter that looked more like a wind-up toy with a propeller. It was indeed a sight to behold.

The 1960s marked a significant milestone in the history of air medical services. The advent of turbine-powered helicopters made air medical transport faster and more efficient. It was similar to upgrading from a tricycle to a Harley Davidson. The speedier helicopters allowed rapid emergency response, reducing travel time for critical patients.

The 1970s saw the emergence of dedicated air medical programs, with hospitals and organizations recognizing the potential of air transport for saving lives. The "HEMS" (Helicopter Emergency Medical Services) concept became increasingly common, and air medical services expanded their reach to provide critical care in remote areas.

Fast-tracking to the present day, and air medical services have become integral to emergency healthcare systems worldwide. Advanced helicopters and fixed-wing aircraft are equipped with state-of-the-art medical equipment and staffed by skilled medical professionals. They can reach patients in remote areas, navigate through challenging weather conditions, and even perform life-saving procedures mid-flight. It's like a medical drama happening in the sky.

Air medical services have come a long way from the days of biplanes and makeshift helicopters. Today, they are a vital component of emergency medical care, providing rapid response and critical care to patients in need.

In the skies, angels of mercy soar, bridging the gap between life and death with each flight, proving that miracles have wings.

EMS Protocols

From the days when a friendly pat on the back passed for CPR to the era of smartphones guiding paramedics' every move, the history of EMS protocols is a ride you won't want to miss!

Our adventure started in ancient times when "EMS protocols" were about as sophisticated as trying to fix a caveman's broken leg with a mammoth tusk. If someone got injured, our ancestors probably just slapped some leaves on the wound and hoped for the best. The "Leave-it-to-Leaves" protocol, shall we?

Now, skipping ahead to the Middle Ages, where things took a more mystical turn. Instead of medical training, it seemed like every village had a local "healer" with a potion for everything from a headache to a plague. Forget evidence-based medicine; this was the "Wizard and Witchcraft" protocol. Who needs science when you've got magic beans, right?

The 19th century brought us the first glimmer of hope. The Red Cross was founded in 1863, and with it came a semblance of order to the chaotic world of emergency response. But don't be fooled; this was still the era of leeches and "bleeding" patients to cure them. Because who wouldn't want to suck the disease right out of you?

The early 20th century saw the birth of modern medicine, and EMS protocols finally started to resemble something remotely scientific. It was like the medical world had just discovered that germs existed.

Ambulances became more than just horse-drawn carriages with a fancy paint job. But it wasn't until the 1960s that we got our first taste of authentic EMS protocols.

As mentioned before, in 1966, the National Highway Traffic Safety Administration (NHTSA) introduced the "Star of Life" symbol, representing the six functions of EMS: detection, reporting, response, on-scene care, care in transit, and transfer to definitive care. It was a road map for EMS protocols.

The '70s saw the birth of "EMT" – Emergency Medical Technician – as a recognized profession. It was like the dawn of a new age, where EMS providers were no longer just glorified ambulance drivers. They were bona fide healthcare professionals, armed with more than just a first-aid kit and a box of Band-Aids.

Leaping forward to today, where EMS protocols have evolved into something far beyond leaves and wizards. Paramedics now have smartphones loaded with apps that guide them through every step of patient care. It resembles having a medical encyclopedia, a GPS, and a life-saving sidekick all in one handy device.

The history of EMS protocols is a journey filled with laughter, tears, and more than a few facepalms. From leaves to smartphones, we've come a long way in our quest to save lives. So, the next time you see a paramedic consulting their smartphone for guidance, remember that it's not just a device; it's a symbol of progress, knowledge, and the ever-evolving world of emergency medical services.

EMS protocols are the compass that guides care, ensuring that every life-saving decision is rooted in knowledge and compassion.

CPR

Cardiopulmonary resuscitation more commonly known as CPR. Where Stayin' Alive is more than just a song. From chest thumps that could double as a tribal dance to the modern miracle of hands-only CPR, it's a life-saving venture worth the hype.

Our tale begins in the 1700s, where CPR was essentially non-existent. If someone keeled over, you'd probably just give them a good shake and shout, "Wake up, you lazy bum!" But the idea of reviving the dearly departed didn't really pick up steam until the 18th century. In 1740, The Paris Academy of Sciences dabbled in the dark arts of "mouth-to-mouth" resuscitation on animals. It's on par with auditioning for a role in a surreal circus.

Over 200 years later, in the 1960s, CPR finally started resembling something we'd recognize today. The American Heart Association (AHA) introduced the "ABC" approach – Airway, Breathing, Compressions. The birth of the CPR alphabet, people could now try to remember their ABCs while saving lives. They even added a catchy tune, "Staying Alive" by the Bee Gees, to help keep the rhythm during compressions. Who knew disco would have such life-saving potential?

The 1960s brought us a real game-changer – the automated external defibrillator (AED) invention. These nifty devices shocked the heart back to life, giving chest compressions a much-needed sidekick, ready to zap life into the party.

But hold onto your defibrillator paddles because the real revolution came in the 2000s with "hands-only CPR." Forget mouth-to-mouth, folks; it's all about the chest thumps! This modern approach ditched the breathing part and focused solely on high-quality chest compressions. No more worrying about what your CPR partner had for lunch. It was like CPR's way of saying, "Breathe if you must, but don't forget the 'thump-thump.'"

Hands-only CPR simplified the life-saving process, making it accessible to more people. You didn't need to be a certified CPR expert to potentially save a life; you just needed the beat of "Stayin' Alive" and the will to push hard and fast on someone's chest. It was like the KISS principle (Keep It Simple, Stupid) for CPR – and we mean that in the most endearing way possible.

Today, hands-only CPR is the rockstar of resuscitation techniques. It's all about the chest compressions, baby! And if you're wondering whether it works, the answer is a resounding "yes." When applied early and correctly, hands-only CPR can double or even triple a person's chances of survival after sudden cardiac arrest.

The history of CPR is a roller coaster of chest thumps and disco beats. From the primitive days of animal mouth-to-mouth experiments to the hands-only CPR revolution, it's a life-saving dance that has evolved.

The history of CPR is a symphony of hands and hearts, the rhythm of life sustained through skill and determination.

The AED

Prepare to be electrified – not literally, of course – as we delve into the shocking history of defibrillators. From clunky contraptions that required a degree in electrical engineering to the modern marvels known as automated external defibrillators (AEDs), it's a story that will make your heart skip a beat – but in a good way.

Our electrifying story started in the late 19th century when electricity was still a mysterious force that could make your hair stand on end. In 1899, two doctors named Jean-Louis Prévost and Frédéric Batelli decided to zap the heart back to life using a crude defibrillator that resembled a pair of salad tongs with wires attached. We think they raided their kitchen drawer for medical equipment!

Then, in the 1930s, we entered the "truly shocking" defibrillator era, thanks to Dr. Claude Beck. He introduced the first direct-current (D.C.) defibrillator. This massive machine required an electrical socket the size of a walrus. Picture a scene from a sci-fi B-movie: doctors frantically cranking up the voltage while shouting, "Clear!" as sparks flew. Shocking, indeed!

The 1950s brought us the next electrifying chapter, with the development of the first closed-chest defibrillator. No more cutting open the patient's chest to access the heart – a significant improvement, if you ask us. These defibrillators looked like bulky briefcases with more wires than a spider's web. But hey, progress is progress, right?

Now, jumping to the 1960s, when the AED (automated external defibrillator) made its entrance. It was like the defibrillator's coming-of-age moment. The AED was smaller, portable, and designed for use by non-medical personnel because who needs a medical degree to save a life.

The AED's true breakthrough came in the 1980s when companies like Philips and Heartstream (later acquired by Hewlett-Packard) began manufacturing these life-saving devices. They were like the iPods of defibrillators – sleek, user-friendly, and ready to play the "shock and roll" game.

Today, AEDs are found everywhere – schools, airports, shopping malls – you name it. They're practically the lifeguards of the digital age, standing by, ready to perform a life-saving intervention with a reassuring voice guiding you through the process. It's almost as if having a personal CPR coach in a box.

The real genius of AEDs lies in their ability to analyze a person's heart rhythm and deliver an electric shock if needed, like having a mini-Einstein inside the device, making split-second decisions that could mean the difference between life and, well, the alternative.

From salad tongs with wires to sleek AEDs that can fit in your backpack, it's a story of innovation, simplicity, and the quest to save lives with a jolt of electricity. So, the next time you see an AED hanging on the wall, think it's not just a box; it's a symbol of how far we've come in the electrifying world of medical technology. Shockingly impressive, wouldn't you say?

With the invention of the AED, we placed the power to restart a heart in the hands of everyday heroes.

Paramedics

G rab your stethoscopes and jump into the back of the ambulance because we're about to embark on a thrilling journey through the history of paramedicine. From the days when "ambulance drivers" doubled as sandwich delivery guys to the highly skilled heroes we have today.

Back in the 1960s, pre-hospital care was about as organized as a kindergarten art class. Back then, if you called for an ambulance, you'd likely get a few folks who knew how to drive but couldn't tell a femur from a fibula. These were the so-called "ambulance attendants" or "ambulance drivers." Their medical expertise probably extended to administering a Band-Aid or offering a comforting pat on the back. Picture them saying, "Don't worry, we've got a Band-Aid for your gunshot wound!"

But in 1969, Los Angeles changed the game by introducing the term "paramedic." These were not just ambulance drivers but skilled medical professionals with specialized training. Paramedics could start I.V.s, administer medications, perform advanced life-saving procedures, and read EKGs like they were deciphering hieroglyphics.

In 1973, the National Registry of Emergency Medical Technicians (NREMT) set national standards for EMS providers, including EMTs

(Emergency Medical Technicians) and paramedics. EMTs received a more basic training, while paramedics underwent comprehensive education and training.

EMTs are the backbone of pre-hospital care. They provide essential first aid, perform CPR, and stabilize patients. Think of them as the calm and steady hand guiding you through the initial phases of an emergency.

Paramedics, on the other hand, are the high-octane response team. They undergo rigorous training, including advanced life support techniques and complex medical procedures. They make split-second decisions that can mean the difference between life and death. Paramedics are the ones you want when things get seriously chaotic.

Today, EMTs and paramedics work together as an inseparable team, each with a unique role. EMTs provide initial care and support, while paramedics swoop with advanced medical interventions when needed. It's a harmonious partnership where one complements the other like a perfectly choreographed dance.

The history of paramedics is a testament to the evolution of pre-hospital care. These dedicated professionals have come a long way from the days of ambulance attendants. EMTs and paramedics working hand in hand, with their distinct roles making the difference between life and death. They're highly skilled individuals ready to save lives with precision, expertise, and a few dance moves.

Paramedics are the frontline warriors of medicine, their history a story of courage and innovation, saving lives one call at a time.

MCIs

The thrilling world of MCIs (Mass Casualty Incidents): These chaotic events bring together more action than a Hollywood blockbuster, with a dash of organized chaos that would make a circus ringmaster proud.

Beginning with a bang, or more accurately, with the heart-stopping realization that something significant has gone down. MCIs don't announce their arrival with polite knocking; they barge in like an uninvited guest at a party. Picture a massive accident, a natural disaster, or an unexpected event that suddenly overwhelms the local healthcare system.

The history of MCIs is as old as humanity itself. Think back to ancient times when plagues, wars, and natural disasters left scores of injured people in their wake. There were no emergency response teams with flashing lights and catchy sirens back then. Just a lot of people screaming, praying, and trying to make sense of the chaos. Much like a Taylor Swift concert.

Fast forward to the 20th century, when the world saw a surge in technological advancements, including transportation and communication. While these developments improved our quality of life, they also made MCIs more complex. Suddenly, you had car pile-ups on highways, train derailments, and plane crashes that involved not just dozens, but hundreds of casualties.

MCI response strategies evolved in tandem with these challenges. Emergency services started developing plans to deal with large-scale disasters. The Incident Command System (ICS), born in the 1970s, became the backbone of managing MCIs. It's like the ultimate organizational playbook, helping first responders coordinate their efforts when the world goes haywire.

But here's the kicker: MCIs are like snowflakes – no two are exactly alike. They can range from a massive earthquake that devastates a city to a train derailment that spills hazardous materials. Responders must be as adaptable as chameleons, ready to tackle whatever chaos the MCI throws at them.

The beauty (or madness) of MCIs lies in the sheer number of moving parts. You've got first responders racing to the scene, triage stations set up to categorize patients based on the severity of their injuries, and hospitals bracing for an influx of casualties. It's like a high-stakes chess game played in real-time, with no winner in sight.

And let's not forget the heroes behind the scenes – the emergency management teams, emergency dispatchers, and healthcare workers who train tirelessly to ensure that when chaos strikes, there's a method to the madness. It's a symphony of organized chaos, with each player knowing their role in the grand production.

MCIs are the harrowing moments when the world turns upside down, and chaos reigns supreme. But they're also a testament to the resilience and adaptability of the human spirit. With history as their teacher, first responders and emergency services have honed their skills to manage the most complex MCIs, much like a well-planned jewelry heist going off without a hitch. Heroes, ready to save lives during the madness.

In the face of chaos, EMS responds with unwavering resolve, turning disaster scenes into stories of survival and resilience.

VI

The Caring Chronicles

Get ready to meet the unsung angels of the medical world: nurses. They've rocked some unforgettable uniforms, been there on battlefields, and even ventured into the cosmos. In 'The Caring Chronicles,' we'll traverse the heartwarming history of nursing, from Florence Nightingale's lamp-lit nights to the impact of nursing organizations that made a difference. It's a journey that will remind you that the most extraordinary heroes sometimes wear scrubs and carry compassion as their superpower.

Nursing History

The history of nursing is a tale as old as time, filled with heroes, perplexing practices, and a dash of crazy to keep things lively. It begins in the murky depths of ancient history, where nursing was a bit like a mystical art. Groups of ancient Egyptians chanted incantations and applied strange ointments to heal the sick. That was the birth of nursing, way back in 3000 BC. It's an old version of 'The Mummy,' minus the action sequences.

Leaping forward to ancient Greece, where the famed Hippocrates – the guy who gave us the Hippocratic Oath – was throwing around medical wisdom like confetti. He believed that nursing required not just a magic touch but also knowledge and compassion. It's as if he said, "Hey, let's add a bit of science to this healing thing, shall we?"

The Middle Ages, however, were a bit of a nursing dark age. We had "plague nurses" in Europe who suited up like they were going to war (against germs, that is). They wore creepy-looking masks filled with aromatic herbs to fend off disease. Imagine dressing up like a bird to heal the sick – medieval nursing was an actual masquerade ball.

The 19th century was when nursing got its much-needed facelift, thanks to the iconic Florence Nightingale. In the 1850s, she waltzed into the Crimean War, lamp in hand, and revolutionized healthcare. She brought cleanliness, organization, and a touch of elegance to nursing. Suddenly, nursing was no longer a guessing game but a science. Florence's "Lady with the Lamp" persona was like the first-ever superhero nurse.

Fast forward to the 20th century, when nursing became a sophisticated blend of science and compassion. The invention of antibiotics and modern surgical techniques turned nurses into true healthcare heroes. They went from being Florence's "lamp-bearers" to administering medications, performing surgeries, and delivering babies with the precision of a Swiss watchmaker.

Today, nursing has evolved into a dynamic and highly respected profession. Nurses are healthcare heroes, donning scrubs instead of bird masks and using state-of-the-art equipment to diagnose, treat, and care for patients. They're the guardians of health, the voices of compassion, and the keepers of sanity in a chaotic world of medicine.

In the annals of healthcare, nursing history is the heartbeat of compassion, tracing the journey of caregivers who heal with heart and hands.

Florence Nightingale

Y ou may remember Florence Nightingale from our previous story as the "Lady with the Lamp." But there's more to this historical figure than just her fondness for mood lighting...

We start back in the 19th century when healthcare was more like a baffling maze than a science. Picture a time when hospitals were often grim, unsanitary places where diseases thrived like party animals at a rock concert. In this era, nursing was hardly a respected profession, more like a second-rate occupation for women with limited career choices.

Born on May 12th, 1820, in Florence, Italy, Florence Nightingale was destined for a life far beyond the confines of traditional Victorian expectations. She didn't just defy societal norms; she tossed them aside like an unwanted hand-me-down. Armed with an unbeatable spirit and a passion for statistics (yes, statistics), Florence embarked on a mission to revolutionize healthcare.

Florence Nightingale's star rose to prominence during the Crimean War (1853-1856). In 1854, the British Army and its French allies found themselves embroiled in this military quagmire. But the war wasn't just fought on the battlefield; it was fought in the hospitals, too, and this was where Florence made her mark.

Florence, now famously known as the "Lady with the Lamp," led a team of nurses to Scutari, a British base hospital in Turkey. These nurses were like the Avengers of healthcare; Florence was their fearless leader. Armed with a lamp to light her way through the dimly lit wards, she tended to the wounded with compassion, determination, and a relentless commitment to hygiene.

It wasn't just Florence's soothing presence or her fancy lamp that worked wonders. She introduced revolutionary sanitary measures, emphasizing cleanliness and proper hygiene practices. She said, "Hey, maybe we should stop spreading diseases in hospitals and start, you know, preventing them."

But Florence wasn't just a hands-on nurse. She was a data wizard, too. Collecting meticulous statistics on patient mortality rates, demonstrating that more soldiers died from preventable diseases than battle wounds. She was the Florence Nightingale, not the Florence 'Ignorance Is Bliss' Nightingale.

After the Crimean War, Florence's influence reached far beyond the battlefield. She founded the first-ever nursing school at St. Thomas' Hospital in London in 1860, turning nursing into a respected profession with proper training and education. Imagine being the nurse who had to explain why you didn't wash your hands before performing surgery after Florence Nightingale had championed cleanliness.

Florence's legacy endures to this day. International Nurses Day is celebrated on her birthday, May 12th, in honor of her remarkable contributions to nursing and healthcare. She didn't just change the game; she rewrote the entire rulebook.

Florence Nightingale, the Lady with the Lamp, illuminated the path of nursing with her compassion and dedication to healing.

Clara Barton

While revisiting history, we meet a woman who redefined the term "angel of mercy." Clara Barton wasn't your average 19th-century lady, but the force behind creating the American Red Cross.

In the early 1800s, Clara Barton entered a world where women were expected to be prim, proper, and anything but assertive. Born on December 25th, 1821, in North Oxford, Massachusetts, Clara had other plans. She took one look at societal norms and said, "Nah, I think I'll redefine what it means to be a woman."

Skipping ahead to the American Civil War (1861-1865), a time when the nation was tearing itself apart like a stubborn pair of jeans. Clara Barton wasted no time in rolling up her sleeves and getting her hands dirty. She wasn't content with the role of a delicate flower; she wanted to be in the thick of things, tending to wounded soldiers on the battlefield.

Picture Clara as a real-life superhero, dodging bullets and cannonballs to provide medical aid to the wounded. With her grit and determination, she became known as the "Angel of the Battlefield." She said, "Why be a damsel in distress when you can be the hero?"

But Clara's heroism didn't stop there. She believed in the power of compassion and fought tooth and nail to ensure that medical supplies reached soldiers in need. In 1864, she received permission to travel with the Army of the James, becoming the first woman to lead an expedition to distribute relief supplies in a war zone. If that doesn't earn her a 'No Fear' bumper sticker, what does?

Clara's experiences during the Civil War and the International Red Cross Movement inspired her. In 1881, she founded the American Red Cross. She practically slapped a red cross on the map and said, "Let's make humanitarianism a thing, folks!"

And humanitarianism it became. Clara Barton's American Red Cross went on to provide disaster relief, support to military families, and blood services. She didn't just start an organization; she ignited a legacy of humanitarian aid that continues today.

Clara Barton's story is a testament to her relentless pursuit of what she believed in, even when society expected her to play by different rules. She challenged gender norms, stared down adversity on the battlefield, and reshaped the landscape of humanitarian aid.

Clara Barton, the Angel of the Battlefield, exemplified the courage and unwavering commitment of nurses in times of crisis.

The Caduceus

P repare to be both enlightened and mildly amused as we dive into the curious history of the Caduceus in nursing. This tale is like a medical sitcom, full of unexpected twists, historical mix-ups, and the emblematic symbol that left Florence Nightingale herself scratching her head.

Let's set the stage in ancient Greece, around 500 BC, where the Caduceus debuted as the staff of Hermes, the Greek messenger god. Hermes, a deity more concerned with delivering scrolls than saving lives, had a staff adorned with two serpents. Perhaps he figured he needed extra reptilian assistance to navigate through the traffic jams of Mount Olympus.

Fast forward to ancient Rome, where the Caduceus made a cameo appearance as the emblem of the Roman god Mercury, a near-carbon copy of Hermes. It's as if the Romans decided that if Greece had a staff-wielding messenger god with serpents, they needed one, too.

Now, let's step into the more modern era of healthcare. In the 19th century, the United States Army Medical Corps adopted the Caduceus as its symbol. Here's where the plot thickens (or gets amusingly confusing): they mistook the Caduceus for the staff of Asclepius, the Greek god of medicine.

Asclepius had a staff with a single serpent, representing healing and rejuvenation. Meanwhile, the Caduceus had two serpents and was the symbol of a messenger god. It's comparable to trying to use a pogo stick as a ladder – they're both tall, but one will get you a lot higher than the other.

The mix-up didn't end there. Soon, the Caduceus appeared on nursing badges, uniforms, and even in some medical institutions' logos. It's almost as if nurses decided to join the Caduceus party without checking if it had a valid medical license.

Florence Nightingale, who we've mentioned before, must have raised an eyebrow at this bizarre choice of symbolism. She focused on saving lives and improving healthcare practices, not confusing symbols. If she were here today, she might give the Caduceus a skeptical side-eye and ask, "What exactly does this have to do with nursing?"

In reality, the Caduceus's place in the nursing field is like a case of mistaken identity that's gone on for centuries. Nurses, dedicated to patient care, unwittingly embraced a symbol more suitable for ancient messengers than modern healthcare heroes.

However, let's give the Caduceus a little credit. Despite its identity crisis, it has become an enduring emblem in nursing. It symbolizes a rich history, albeit one of misunderstandings, and the dedication of nurses who, like Florence Nightingale, have been beacons of compassion and healing.

Nurses decided to wear two snakes and a messenger's staff just to keep history on its toes. And while it may not make complete sense, it's a testament to the resilience and adaptability of the nursing profession, even in the face of a symbol with an identity crisis.

The Caduceus symbolizes not just medicine but the compassion and care that nurses bring to the forefront of healthcare.

Nursing During WW1

D iving into the fascinating but often overlooked nursing chapter during World War I, that delightful period in history often dubbed "The Great War." Demonstrating that even in the bleakest of times, nurses can add a touch of greatness.

It's the early 20th century, and the world is in turmoil. The Great War, which raged from 1914 to 1918, was like a global bar brawl on an epic scale. Nations clashed like feuding families at a Thanksgiving dinner gone horribly wrong. But during the chaos and carnage, a group of unsung heroes stepped onto the stage: nurses.

Let's start with a bit of context. As we've already mentioned, nursing was evolving in the years leading up to World War I, thanks to Florence Nightingale. Nursing was no longer just about mopping brows and fluffing pillows; it was a profession with a purpose.

When the war broke out in 1914, nurses worldwide rushed to the front lines. They weren't armed with rifles but with compassion, medical knowledge, and a limitless supply of courage. They said, "Who needs bayonets when you have bandages?"

Picture this: The trenches of World War I were muddy, cramped, and teeming with wounded soldiers. But in the chaos, nurses worked tirelessly. They waded through knee-deep mud, braving bombs and gas attacks to care for the wounded. It was like a never-ending, gruesome episode of 'Nurse Grit and the War Zone.'

Nurses during World War I were exposed to the horrors of modern warfare like no one else. They treated injuries caused by machine guns, chemical weapons, and the sheer brutality of battle. They weren't just nurses but battlefield magicians, using whatever they had to save lives.

But here's the twist: They did all this without the recognition they deserved. While soldiers got medals and parades, nurses often toiled in the shadows, receiving a polite nod for their efforts. Like being the unsung hero in a blockbuster movie, only without the fame and fortune.

Despite the hardships and lack of acknowledgment, nurses persevered. They proved that even in the darkest of times, humanity could shine through. Their dedication and innovations during World War I laid the foundation for modern nursing practices and nurses' vital role in healthcare.

In 1918, when the war finally drew to a close, nurses continued their work. They treated the wounded and played a crucial role in the global recovery process. They decided that the encore was just as important even after the main act was over.

It wasn't just a war of soldiers and generals; it was a war where nurses proved that greatness could emerge from the most unlikely places. They battled not with guns and tanks but with kindness, resilience, and a determination to heal. It might not have been the "Great War" for everyone, but it was an opportunity to make a world of difference for nurses.

In the midst of war's chaos, nurses in World War I stood as beacons of hope, providing healing and solace in the bleakest of times.

Nursing Uniforms

From starched whites that could double as sails to the trendy scrubs that have taken over, the history of nursing attire is a fascinating blend of style and functionality.

In the early 19th century, a time when nursing was more about dedication than fashion statements. Nurses, often nuns, were found clad in long, flowing dresses. Picture a combination of Victorian-era modesty and a tad bit of theatrical flair. These early nurses could have doubled as extras in a period drama with their bonnets and floor-length gowns.

Then, in Florence Nightingale's era in the mid-1800s. The "Lady with the Lamp" was all about cleanliness and order, and she advocated for a more practical nursing uniform. Hence, the classic white uniform was born. It was crisp, starched, and spotless as a blank canvas – perfect for painting the future of modern nursing.

The early 20th century saw the emergence of the iconic nurse's cap. A symbol of pride and authority, these caps were so starched and structured that they could double as a handy desk organizer in a pinch. The hats perched atop nurses' heads like fluffy crowns, instantly distinguishing them from mere mortals.

But, as time marched on, so did nursing attire. By the 1960s, the cap was losing its luster. The uniform underwent a revolution of its own, shedding the stiff collars and adopting a more relaxed look. Nursing dresses became shorter, a nod to the ever-evolving world of fashion. Nursing decided to join the swinging '60s party.

The '70s and '80s saw a remarkable shift towards comfort. Polyester scrubs started to gain ground. They were colorful, practical, and, yes, a tad disco-infused. If the '70s were all about "Saturday Night Fever," nurses were ready to dance their shifts away.

Here we are in the 21st century, where nursing uniforms have embraced the scrubs revolution wholeheartedly. Gone are the days of starched whites and towering caps. Modern scrubs are all about functionality, with pockets to carry everything from stethoscopes to snacks. And the colors! Nursing scrubs come in a rainbow of choices, from calming blues to neon pinks, ensuring nurses are ready for any fashion emergency.

Why the shift? Well, in a world where nursing is about more than just appearances, scrubs make perfect sense. They're comfortable and hygienic and allow nurses to move with ease. And let's not forget the stylish accessories that modern nurses can add to their outfits – from funky compression socks to personalized badge reels. It's similar to them, combining fashion and function in a fabulous blend.

Nursing uniforms have evolved from billowing gowns to sleek scrubs to match the changing times. They might not be walking down fashion runways, but nurses sure know how to rock those scrubs like runway models. Fashion-forward and practical – that's the modern nursing uniform for you!

Nursing uniforms are more than attire; they are a symbol of dedication, a cape of compassion worn by everyday heroes.

The Impact of Nursing Organizations

Hold onto your stethoscopes as we uncover the secret world of nursing organizations, where nurses don capes and wield policy papers instead of swords. These organizations, like the American Nurses Association (ANA) and the International Council of Nurses (ICN), have been quietly shaping the nursing profession and influencing healthcare policies.

In 1896, the ANA was founded. Nurses in their starched whites gathered around a table like a scene from "The Talk." They didn't have smartphones or social media; they had determination and a shared mission. They said, "Let's form an organization to advocate for nursing and healthcare!" And so, the ANA was born, ready to take on the world.

Over the years, the ANA became the voice of American nurses, advocating for improved working conditions, higher education standards, and, most importantly, a seat at the healthcare decision-making table. They lobbied for nurses like no one's business, ensuring they had a say in policies affecting their daily lives. They had a direct hotline to Capitol Hill, with nurses whispering in the ears of lawmakers.

Meanwhile, the ICN was flexing its nursing muscles on the global stage. Founded in 1899, it was the ANA's international cousin. Nurses from different corners of the world came together to say, "Hey, let's unite, share knowledge, and improve healthcare worldwide!" Like the Avengers of Nursing, without the flashy costumes and Hollywood budgets.

The ICN championed nursing standards, ethics, and education glob-ally. They played a pivotal role in advancing nursing as a respected profession, not just in the U.S. but around the world.

The ANA and ICN have been the driving force behind many healthcare policies that affect us all. From advocating for better patient care to pushing for safer working conditions, they've been on the frontlines, even if those frontlines were often conference rooms and committee meetings.

In recent years, their influence has only grown. They've tackled issues like nurse staffing ratios, healthcare access, and the role of nurse practitioners. They've gone from bedside care to bedside advocacy, ensuring that nurses have a voice in shaping the future of healthcare.

These organizations may not have capes or superpowers. Still, they're the backbone of the nursing profession, fighting for the rights and well-being of nurses and patients alike. Like having a guardian angel in a business suit, tirelessly working to improve healthcare.

Nursing organizations unite the profession, amplifying the voices of caregivers, and shaping the future of healthcare.

Nurse Practitioners

As mentioned earlier, the nurse practitioner's role has developed over time. It was an incredible journey from humble beginnings to their current status as healthcare superheroes. Our story unfolds in the mid-20th century when the healthcare landscape was like a perplexing maze of specialties and subspecialties. Enter the nurse practitioners, a breed of healthcare professionals with one foot in nursing and the other in medicine. It's like they said, "Why choose one when we can have both?"

In the 1960s, nurse practitioners emerged as a beacon of hope amid a shortage of primary care physicians. They were the original multitaskers, seamlessly blending their nursing skills with advanced clinical training to provide a wide range of healthcare services. They wore capes under their scrubs and said, "Fear not, we've got this!"

Nurse practitioners were like the Swiss Army knives of healthcare, diagnosing, treating, and educating patients with a level of care and attention that made everyone else look like amateurs. By the 1970s, they had firmly established themselves as primary care providers. They'd staked their claim on the healthcare frontier, saying, "Move over, traditional medicine, there's a new sheriff in town."

As the years went by, nurse practitioners continued to evolve. They diversified into various specialties, from family medicine to pediatrics and even acute care. They were collecting superhero capes, one specialization at a time. They didn't just provide care; they delivered it with a side of empathy and understanding that made patients feel genuinely seen and heard.

In the 21st century, nurse practitioners stepped into the limelight, advocating for policies that expanded their scope of practice. They fought battles and faced skepticism but ultimately prevailed, gaining recognition as essential members of the healthcare team.

Their ability to connect with patients on a personal level is second to none. Nurse practitioners are renowned for their bedside manner, treating patients not just as medical cases but as individuals with unique stories and needs. They have a PhD in compassion.

They've come a long way from their modest beginnings in the mid-20th century, and they're here to stay. Nurse practitioners are the embodiment of healthcare excellence, proving that a combination of nursing know-how and medical expertise can indeed save the day, one patient at a time.

Nurse practitioners are the bridge between science and empathy, offering holistic care that heals both body and soul.

Nursing Medical Breakthroughs

Nurses have made remarkable contributions to medical innovations. From defying stereotypes to bending the boundaries of healthcare, nurses have left their indelible mark on history.

The story begins in the 19th century, a time when nursing was more about fluffing pillows than redefining healthcare. A familiar name comes up: Florence Nightingale, who, as we know, in the mid-1800s, decided to challenge the status quo. She revolutionized patient care by introducing hygiene practices, sanitation improvements, and even statistical analysis.

Fast forward to the early 20th century, and we have the intrepid nurse Lillian Wald. She pioneered public health nursing, establishing the Henry Street Settlement in New York City. Wald didn't wait for patients to come to her; she went to them, delivering healthcare to underserved communities. She was the original UberEats but for healthcare.

In the 1950s, ambitious nurse Sister Mary Kenneth Keller didn't just break glass ceilings; she smashed them to smithereens. She became one of the first women to earn a Ph.D. in computer science. She went on to develop the computer programming language BASIC. So, the next time you're annoyed by a computer glitch, remember to thank a nurse. It's reminiscent of healing both humans and machines.

In the 1960s, nurse Evelyn Lundeen pushed the envelope with the invention of the crash cart, which contained life-saving medications and emergency equipment. She took the idea of "house calls" to a whole new level, ensuring help was never too far away, even in the most critical situations.

Jumping ahead again to the 1980s, when nurse Nancy Wood invented the first fetal heart monitor. This device allowed healthcare providers to monitor the heartbeats of unborn babies, ensuring their well-being during pregnancy and labor. She brought the stethoscope into the womb, keeping an ear on the next generation.

But the innovations didn't stop there. In recent years, nurses have been at the forefront of healthcare technology, designing and implementing electronic health records (EHRs) that have streamlined patient care. Turning medical records into digital gold mines of information, accessible at the touch of a button.

Beneath the scrubs is a mind brimming with innovation. From Florence Nightingale's hygiene practices to Sister Mary Kenneth Keller's code, nurses are heroes of healthcare progress. They've taken healthcare by storm, breaking barriers and introducing innovations that have transformed the field. Nurses aren't just caregivers but inventors, pioneers, and champions of a healthier world.

In the quest for medical breakthroughs, nurses are the silent heroes, driving innovation and changing lives one discovery at a time.

Nursing In Space

P repare to embark on a celestial journey as we explore the fascinating realm of nursing in space. Yep, nurses have boldly ventured beyond Earth's atmosphere to provide healthcare support to astronauts and conduct mind-boggling medical research in the vacuum of space.

Our tale began in the early days of space exploration when astronauts were venturing into the great unknown with little more than duct tape and a prayer. It was the 1960s, and nurses like Dolores O'Hara and Dee O'Hara (yes, two remarkable O'Haras!) played a vital role in astronaut care. They ensured that astronauts were in peak physical condition and mentally prepared for their space odysseys. They were the original personal trainers but with a zero-gravity twist.

In 1973, Skylab, America's first space station, took nurses to new heights—literally. Nurse Dee O'Hara (yes, she's back) joined the Skylab Medical Team, proving that nurses weren't just earthbound healers. They were celestial caregivers, too. Their scrubs were ready for liftoff!

Nurses also played a part in the space shuttle era in the 1980s. Nurse Bonnie Dunbar, an astronaut herself, was instrumental in developing medical kits for space missions. Imagine designing a medical kit that can handle everything from interstellar indigestion to space sneezes. Nurses like Bonnie made it happen, "MacGyvering" the cosmos.

In 1991 the ultimate nursing accolade arrived when Eileen Collins became the first female Space Shuttle pilot. She didn't just break the glass ceiling; she launched herself through it at Mach 25! Eileen proved that nurses could conquer gravity and defy stereotypes and preconceptions. She said, "Nurses can navigate the final frontier, too!"

And then there's the remarkable research conducted by nurses in space. In 2001, Karen Nyberg, a NASA astronaut and nurse, conducted experiments on the International Space Station (ISS) to study the effects of microgravity on the human body. She turned the ISS into a floating laboratory, conducting cosmic experiments with a side of zero-gravity physics.

But nursing in space isn't just about being healthcare heroes to astronauts; it's about pushing the boundaries of medical science. Researchers like Dr. Cheryl Nickerson have studied how microgravity impacts bacterial virulence, potentially leading to groundbreaking discoveries in disease treatment back on Earth. Turning space into a petri dish, with microbes conducting their own cosmic experiments.

Nurses have not only touched lives on Earth but have also ventured into the great unknown to care for astronauts and advance medical knowledge. They've taken healthcare to new heights. Nurses are the cosmic caregivers, proving that their skills and expertise are not bound by gravity or even the limits of our atmosphere. They've shown us that when it comes to nursing, the sky is not the limit; it's just the beginning of an infinite universe of possibilities.

In the final frontier, nurses continue to reach for the stars, proving that even in space, compassion knows no bounds.

VII

Military Marvels

Prepare for a salute-worthy tour through the history of the U.S. military, where ranks are as complicated as a complex puzzle, tanks are more rigid than an unbreakable wall, and innovation is the order of the day. 'Military Marvels' invites you to explore America's armed forces past, present, and future, with a generous sprinkling of humor along the way. Whether it's learning about medals, the evolution of uniforms, or the incredible innovations that shaped history, get ready for a journey.

History of the U.S. Military

O nce upon a time, in a land known as the United States of America, a military force was born. It all began on a chilly day in 1775 when a bunch of folks decided they needed a group of tough cookies to protect their newly declared independence from the British Empire. And so, on November 10th, the Marine Corps was born, becoming the oldest branch of the U.S. military. They were like the cool older siblings of the American military family.

Not too long after, in 1776, some really smart folks gathered in Philadelphia and penned the Declaration of Independence. This was basically a breakup letter to King George III. The British didn't take it too well, so they sent their troops across the Atlantic to crash the party. Cue the American Revolutionary War! It kicked off in earnest in 1775 (yeah, the same year as the Marine Corps' birthday), but things got real in 1776. George Washington led the Continental Army into battle with his stylish powdered wig. It wasn't always pretty, but they managed to pull off a victory and become a new nation.

A few decades later, in the 19th century, The United States grew like a teenager, hitting a growth spurt. In 1812, they decided to take on their former British foes again in the aptly named War of 1812. This war saw the burning of the White House and the inspiration for a catchy national anthem, "The Star-Spangled Banner."

Then, in the 1860s, the country found itself in a bit of a family feud

– the American Civil War. This was a classic case of "brother against brother," which raged from 1861 to 1865. The Union Army donned in blue, and the Confederate Army, with their signature gray uniforms, duked it out in America's deadliest conflict. It ended with the Union victorious.

The late 1800s brought a dash of westward expansion and some skirmishes with Native American tribes. Not the brightest moments in American history, but let's not dwell on that. Instead, let's jump forward to 1917, when the U.S. decided to join the party in World War I. The doughboys, as the American troops were called, headed to Europe and helped tip the balance in favor of the Allies.

Then came the roaring '20s, but things got rough in the '30s. The Great Depression hit, and that wasn't fun for anyone. But don't worry, the '40s were just around the corner, and they brought a doozy of a World War – World War II, to be precise. Pearl Harbor got a rude awakening in 1941 when Japan decided to drop in unannounced. The U.S. wasn't having it, and they joined the Allies once again. D-Day, Hiroshima, and Nagasaki were all on the menu, and the war ended with the U.S. dropping the mic (and the atomic bomb) in 1945.

The Cold War, a not-so-hot conflict with the Soviet Union, kept things interesting for the next few decades. Korea and Vietnam were like the appetizers before the main course of the Cold War – the Cuban Missile Crisis. The world held its breath, hoping the U.S. and the Soviets wouldn't press that big red button.

Skipping ahead to the 21st century, the U.S. military has been busy in places like Iraq and Afghanistan, dealing with the aftermath of 9/11. Today, the U.S. military is like the big brother on the world stage, with a history filled with battles, victories, and moments that make you scratch your head and say, "Well, that happened."

The story of the U.S. military is a tale of bravery, innovation, and a whole lot of drama on the world stage. From its humble beginnings in

1775 to its current role as a global superpower, it's a story that keeps on evolving, one chapter at a time.

The history of the U.S. military is a saga of sacrifice, valor, and unwavering commitment to safeguarding the ideals of freedom.

U.S. Military Ranks

I n the land of stars, stripes, and a whole lot of military might, the United States found itself in need of some order among its brave souls in uniform. Thus, the hierarchy of military ranks was born, and oh boy, has it evolved like a chameleon at a color-changing convention!

Let's dial back to the American Revolution. In those early days, the Continental Army was not unlike a bunch of folks deciding to play soldier in their backyard. There were hardly any ranks, and people just sort of did their own thing. You had your generals and your privates and little in between. After all, they were fighting the British; there was no time for formalities.

But as America grew up and realized it needed a proper military, it adopted a rank structure inspired by its European counterparts. In 1775, George Washington, the O.G. of American generals, became the Continental Army's Commander-in-Chief. He set the standard with his three-star insignia. Yes, three stars – because he was just that good.

By 1798, the U.S. Navy decided to join the party and introduced its own ranks. The good ol' Army and Navy couldn't agree on a standard set of ranks, so they went their separate ways. Ah, sibling rivalry.

Fast forward to 1861, and the Civil War was in full swing. The Union and Confederate armies adopted similar rank structures, with your standard officers like captains, majors, and colonels leading the charge.

Following them, of course, you had the generals, who were like the rock stars of the battlefield.

But the fun was just getting started. After the Civil War, the military decided to add some bling to their uniforms. Suddenly, we had First Lieutenants, Second Lieutenants, and more. It was like a rank buffet, and everyone piled their plates high.

The 20th century brought even more changes. In 1947, the Department of Defense was created, and they decided to standardize the ranks across all branches. No more Army and Navy doing their own thing. Now, everyone would play by the same rank rules.

Here's where things get interesting. The Air Force was officially established as a separate branch in 1947 (previously, it was part of the Army), and they decided to get all fancy with their ranks. Instead of your typical private or corporal, they introduced Airman Basic, Airman First Class, and all sorts of other "air-tastic" titles. Because, you know, flying high in the sky deserves some extra flair.

Nowadays, the U.S. military has a rank structure that resembles an alphabet soup. It's a veritable ranking buffet from E-1 (Private) to O-10 (four-star General/Admiral). And let's remember those Warrant Officers who lurk in the shadows with their unique brand of expertise.

So there you have it, the history of the U.S. military ranks in all its glory. It's evolved from the wildest days of the American Revolution to the standardized system we have today. And in case you're wondering, yes, we still have generals and admirals with enough stars to light up the night sky.

In the hierarchy of service, ranks are not just badges but a reflection of character, competence, and leadership.

U.S. Military Branches

The captivating tale of the United States military branches – a saga of sibling rivalry, bureaucratic bungles, and the occasional stroke of genius.

It's the 18th century, and the American colonies feel a little rebellious. The Continental Congress, in its infinite wisdom, decided it needed some organized muscle to take on the British. So, in 1775, they birthed the Continental Army, the very first of the military branches, with George Washington donning his fanciest three-star general hat.

Then, "re-enter" stage left in 1789, and the United States Marine Corps was re-established. These folks decided to be different and introduced their unique ranks, like "Lance Corporal" and "Sergeant Major," just to keep things interesting. Because why go with the conventional when you can be the quirky cousin of the military family?

Moving along to 1794, when the U.S. Navy weighed anchor and set sail as an official branch. Sailors in those days were a hardy bunch, dealing with everything from pirates to sea monsters (or so they claimed). And, of course, they brought their own set of ranks, setting the stage for some good ol' fashioned inter-branch competition.

Now, the 19th century was like a coming-of-age montage for the U.S. military. It got its act together, dressed up in proper uniforms, and started acting like a grown-up military power... Sort of... The Civil War was a bit of a family feud, with the Army battling the Army. Still, it helped cement the military as a key player in American history.

Then, in the 20th century, they brought even more additions to our military smorgasbord. In 1947, the Air Force decided to spread its wings and become a separate branch. And don't forget the Coast Guard, always creeping in the background, ready to save stranded sailors and confiscate illegal cargo. Established as an official branch in 1915, they keep the shores safe while the other branches do their land and air thing.

Then, a tale of cosmic proportions – the creation of the Space Force. A move that had some folks scratching their heads and others reaching for their tinfoil hats. This space-age branch blasted off on December 20th, 2019, as the newest addition to the U.S. military family. Forget about ships, tanks, and boots on the ground; the Space Force's mission is to boldly go where no branch has gone before. They're here to protect us from aliens, rogue satellites, and perhaps even the occasional cosmic hiccup.

Today, our military branches stand proudly side by side, each with its own unique history, culture, and, of course, rivalries. You've got the Army, the oldest and the biggest. The Navy, with its timeless sea shanties and maritime lore. The Marines, the tough cookies with their distinctive ranks. The Air Force, reaching for the skies. And the Coast Guard, our unsung heroes of the high seas. And we can't forget the newest member, the out of this world, Space Force.

United in purpose, diverse in specialties, the branches of the U.S. military form a symphony of strength in defense of the nation.

U.S. Military Uniforms

P repare to embark through time, exploring the fascinating and, at times, fashion-challenged history of U.S. military uniforms. The saga begins in the late 1700s, a time when powdered wigs were still all the rage, and muskets were considered high-tech weaponry.

Back in the Revolutionary War era, the Continental Army sported uniforms that were a mishmash of styles and colors. There were some snazzy blue coats with red trimmings, but you could also find soldiers in everything from brown to green. It was a colonial fashion free-for-all, with each regiment adding its own flair to the mix.

Jumping ahead to the early 1800s, the Army decided it needed a little more pizzazz. In 1812, they introduced the iconic blue uniform with bright buttons, tall shakos (those fancy hats with feathers), and self-indulgence. It was the military's attempt at high fashion. But they didn't stop there; they even tried white uniforms in the summer. Nothing says practicality like a uniform that's a magnet for dirt.

By the time the Civil War rolled around in the 1860s, both the Union and Confederate armies had traded their colorful uniforms for something a bit more practical – drab, earth-toned attire. Who had time for fancy outfits when you were too busy fighting brother against brother?

The late 19th century saw the introduction of khaki uniforms, perfect for blending in with sandy environments during the Spanish-American

War. And if you think military fashion was immune to trends, think again! In 1902, the Army ditched its beloved blue uniforms for the classic olive drab, a hue that would become synonymous with World War I.

World War II was all about the iconic green and brown Army uniforms, complete with those stylish overseas caps. The Navy stuck with its classic navy blue, while the Marines continued to stand out with their snazzy dress blues. Meanwhile, in its infancy, the Air Force tried to look sharp with their khakis and bomber jackets.

The 1950s introduced camouflage patterns, perfect for blending into the jungles of Korea and later the rice paddies of Vietnam. And don't forget the Navy's introduction of the crackerjack uniform, with its distinctive bell-bottom trousers. This fashion statement could only be described as "nautical chic."

In the 21st century, camouflage has become the go-to pattern for all branches. And the dress uniforms? Well, they're still as fancy as ever, with rows of ribbons and medals that could put a Christmas tree to shame.

Each era has brought its unique style to the battlefield, from colonial mishmashes to khakis, olive drab, and digital camo. And those extravagant dress uniforms because nothing says "I mean business" like a soldier decked out in more bling than a Hollywood starlet.

As we look back on this sartorial story, one can't help but wonder what the future holds for military fashion. Will we see soldiers in spacesuits or holographic camouflage? Only time will tell, but one thing's for sure: the U.S. military will continue to march to the beat of its own, sometimes eccentric, fashion drum.

In the fabric of our nation's history, military uniforms stand as a tapestry woven with honor, duty, and tradition.

U.S. Military Weapons

The history of U.S. military weapons is a riveting journey that spans from musket balls to missiles and, yes, includes some questionable choices along the way.

It was the late 1700s. The American colonies were flexing their newfound independence muscles, and the weapons of choice were muskets, bayonets, and cannons. These early American soldiers were about as accurate as a blindfolded archer at midnight, but hey, it got the job done during the Revolutionary War.

But as America grew, so did its appetite for bigger and better weaponry. Enter the War of 1812, where the U.S. showcased its penchant for hilariously named firearms like the "Brown Bess" musket and the "Pistole Model 1805 Type II." Who needs fancy names when you've got firepower.

Then, during the Civil War, the U.S. military was armed to the teeth with rifled muskets, Gatling guns, and ironclad ships. The Gatling gun, a precursor to the modern machine gun, was like the grandfather of rapid-fire weaponry – a true marvel in its day.

As the 19th century faded into the 20th, World War I introduced us to the Springfield M1903. This bolt-action rifle proved handy for long-range shooting. And not to be forgotten the trench warfare, where soldiers on both sides hunkered down in mud and misery.

World War II was the era of innovation. The M1 Garand, with its iconic "ping" sound when the clip ejected, became the standard-issue rifle for American G.I.s. Meanwhile, the B-17 Flying Fortress and the B-29 Superfortress were like the rock stars of the sky, raining down destruction with bombs that made TNT look like firecrackers.

The Cold War brought us a whole new level of military hardware. The M16 rifle became the go-to firearm for American troops. At the same time, the Navy flexed its nuclear muscles with submarines like the USS Nautilus, the world's first nuclear-powered sub. And who could forget the strategic missiles like the Minutemen and the Polaris, ready to turn the world into one big barbecue if need be?

Now, moving on to Vietnam, where American soldiers were armed with M16s that tended to jam in the humid jungle. A real "winning" choice of weapon, right? And don't even get us started on the flamethrowers. Because nothing says "Welcome to the jungle" like a backpack that spews fire.

The Gulf War introduced us to the M1 Abrams tank and the Patriot missile system, both of which confidently performed their jobs. But wait, we couldn't resist one last quirky choice – the bayonet. Because when you've got tanks and missiles, what better way to end a conflict than with a good old-fashioned charge into battle with a pointy stick?

Today, the U.S. military boasts an impressive arsenal of weaponry, from stealth bombers to unmanned drones. And while we've come a long way from muskets and flamethrowers, the quirky and sometimes questionable choices of the past remind us that even the mightiest military can have its moments of, shall we say, unique decision-making.

Weapons are the tools of defense, but the true strength of the U.S. military lies in the courage and determination of its soldiers.

U.S. Military Vehicles

The history of U.S. military vehicles is one heck of a roller coaster ride. From humble horse-drawn carriages to high-tech tanks, it's a wild journey that will leave you wondering how anyone ever thought some of these contraptions were a good idea.

Let's hop in the time machine and set the dial to the Revolutionary War era. Back then, it was all about the horse-drawn artillery. Soldiers clinging to rickety wooden carriages, trying to aim cannons that seemed about as accurate as a hurricane spaghetti plot. It's a miracle they hit anything at all.

During the Civil War, things got a bit more interesting. Ironclad warships, like the USS Monitor and the CSS Virginia, took to the seas. They were basically floating tanks, complete with massive cannons and iron armor. Meanwhile, the Army was rolling along on land in wagons and horse-drawn ambulances. Who needs horsepower when you've got actual horses?

As the 20th century dawned, so did the era of automobiles. In World War I, we saw the birth of the military truck, the humble battlefield workhorse. These early trucks were about as reliable as a 1980s home computer. Still, they got the job done, transporting troops and supplies to the frontlines.

World War II was the heyday of military vehicles. The Jeep, that iconic symbol of American military might, debuted. It was like the Swiss Army knife of vehicles, capable of everything from reconnaissance to towing heavy artillery. And don't forget the Sherman tank, a true workhorse that rolled through battlefields like a bulldozer with an attitude.

But then came the Korean War, and the military decided to dabble in the weird and wacky. The M29 Weasel, an amphibious tracked vehicle, was like the ugly duckling of military vehicles. It could go anywhere, but it looked like a reject from a sci-fi B-movie.

The Cold War brought us the iconic M60 Patton tank, a beast on treads that could effortlessly churn through mud and snow. Then there's the Bradley Fighting Vehicle, designed to carry troops into the heart of battle while looking like something out of a futuristic action movie.

Then, the Gulf War introduced us to the M1 Abrams tank, a hulking behemoth that could take a hit like a heavyweight boxer and keep on rolling. The Arnold Schwarzenegger of military vehicles, ready to terminate anything in its path.

Today, the U.S. military boasts an impressive fleet of vehicles, from armored Humvees to MRAPs (Mine-Resistant Ambush Protected) that can survive roadside bombs. And not to be outdone, the futuristic F-35 Joint Strike Fighter. This high-tech marvel could shoot down enemy aircraft and make a mean cup of coffee (just kidding, but it does almost everything else).

The history of U.S. military vehicles is bumpy and sometimes baffling. From wooden wagons to high-tech tanks, it's a journey filled with innovation, experimentation, and the occasional head-scratching choice. But one thing is certain: whether on land, sea, or in the air, the U.S. military knows how to roll in style – or at least in something that gets the job done.

From land to sea and air, military vehicles carry the dreams of liberty and the weight of duty into the heart of every mission.

Pearl Harbor and Fort Knox

Gather 'round, folks, as we delve into the intriguing history of two iconic U.S. military bases. We're talking about the kind of places where legends are made, secrets are whispered, and the coffee in the mess hall is strong enough to power a small city.

First up, we have Pearl Harbor Naval Base in Hawaii, a name that sends shivers down the spine of anyone who remembers the fateful date – December 7, 1941. With its picturesque island backdrop and calm waters, this place was the site of one of the most infamous sneak attacks in history. On that day, the Japanese launched a surprise assault that jolted America out of its peaceful slumber and catapulted it into World War II. It was the ultimate wake-up call, courtesy of torpedoes and bombers.

Pearl Harbor's history is a roller coaster ride of fortifications, battleships, and top-secret operations. The military's version of a "choose your own adventure" novel, with twists and turns at every corner. Pearl Harbor has seen everything from the construction of massive dry docks in the early 20th century to the top-secret code-breaking operations that led to victory in the Pacific theater.

Now, let's hop over to the East Coast and land at the doorstep of Fort Knox, Kentucky. If you've ever heard the phrase "as secure as Fort Knox," you know this place means business. It's the kind of fortress where they store things that make Scrooge McDuck's money bin look like chump change. We're talking about gold – lots and lots of it.

Fort Knox's history is like a tale of buried treasure, minus the pirate ships and X-marks-the-spot maps. It became the U.S. Bullion Depository in 1937; from then on, it was like the Pentagon's piggy bank. With layers of security that make Alcatraz look like a summer camp, Fort Knox guards over 147 million ounces of gold worth billions upon billions of dollars. It's the kind of place where even James Bond would have trouble breaking in.

But Fort Knox isn't just about gold; it's a military base with a rich history of tank warfare. It served as a training ground for armored divisions during World War II, turning raw recruits into tank-driving, tank-fighting machines. It's like the birthplace of American tank warfare, where Sherman tanks rumbled through the training grounds like mechanical beasts of war.

The enthralling histories of two of the most iconic U.S. military bases. Pearl Harbor, with its tragic but pivotal role in history, and Fort Knox, the impregnable fortress that safeguards a mountain of gold. These places are like time capsules of American military might, where the past meets the present and where legends are born – often with a side of intrigue and a sprinkle of mystery.

Pearl Harbor and Fort Knox are the echoes of history, where bravery met adversity, and resilience guarded our nation's treasures.

U.S. Military Medals

Our journey through the fascinating world of U.S. military medals takes us on a historical roller coaster, from the heart-shaped Badge of Military Merit during the American Revolution to the 20th century, where medals multiplied like rabbits.

Our journey began during the American Revolution when the Continental Congress decided it was high time to recognize the brave souls fighting for independence. In 1782, they introduced the Badge of Military Merit, a heart-shaped medal with purple silk and a dash of patriotism. But here's the kicker – it was awarded for "unusual gallantry" and could be exchanged for a warm fuzzy feeling. Just kidding, it was exchanged for cold, hard cash.

Moving ahead to 1847, during the Mexican-American War frenzy, someone came up with a "certificate of merit" – because, you know, nothing says 'thanks for risking your life' like a piece of paper. Oh, and don't worry, there was no fancy medal to go with it. After the war, they must've realized just how valuable those pieces of paper were because they promptly discontinued the whole charade.

Now, talking about the Civil War, a time when military medals were popping up like daisies. The Army Medal of Honor Act of 1862 birthed the Medal of Honor as we know it today.

The late 19th and early 20th centuries saw a flurry of medal mania. The Spanish-American War brought us the Spanish Campaign Medal, the

Dewey Medal, and the Sampson Medal — because why have one medal when you can have three? Then, the Distinguished Service Cross (DSC), the second-highest military decoration awarded for valor. Because when you're not quite Medal of Honor material, there's always a silver medal to strive for.

In World War 1, they decided to grace us with the Distinguished Service Medal (DSM), awarded for "exceptionally meritorious service to the government" — because who needs specifics, right? Unlike that pesky DSC mentioned earlier, which is only given for those trivial combat actions, the DSM was here to show that you could be exceptionally meritorious anywhere, anytime, no combat required. Because why restrict recognition to those who risk their lives in the thick of battle when you can celebrate exceptional merit in the office, the mess hall, or anywhere else for that matter?

The 20th century was like the jackpot for medals. The Purple Heart (again), the Bronze Star, the Silver Star — it was like a medal bonanza. They also upped the medal game by creating the Air Medal, the Soldier's Medal, and the Navy and Marine Corps Medal — because everyone deserves a participation trophy, right? And don't forget the introduction of the Bronze Star Medal with a "V" device for valor because sometimes you just need a little extra bling on your bling.

The Cold War brought us medals like the Armed Forces Expeditionary Medal and the National Defense Service Medal. You never know when you might need a trophy just for showing up. And let's not forget the "V" device for the Meritorious Service Medal because sometimes meritorious service just isn't enough.

Today, U.S. military medals come in all shapes and sizes, recognizing everything from combat heroics to good behavior. So, remember that each medal tells a story of valor, service, and sometimes, just a touch of good old-fashioned bureaucratic bling.

Military medals are not just decorations; they are the embodiment of valor, sacrifice, and the indomitable spirit of those who serve.

U.S. Military Innovations

U.S. military innovations – a story of brilliant breakthroughs, curious experiments, and the occasional "What were they thinking?" moments.

The American Revolution when the Founding Fathers decided they needed a bang for their buck. They devised the "Puckle Gun," a weapon that could fire both round bullets and square shots (yep, square shots). It was like the all-in-one of firearms, except it didn't quite catch on, possibly because soldiers couldn't figure out how to load the darn thing in the heat of battle.

Leaping ahead to the Civil War, we witnessed the birth of military innovations like the Gatling Gun. This hand-cranked, multi-barreled monstrosity could spit out bullets faster than a toddler can empty a candy jar. It was the early version of the minigun and it made mincemeat out of enemy lines. And the unforgettable Confederates' attempt at innovation with the "CSS Hunley," a submarine with a knack for sinking itself more often than the enemy.

As the 20th century dawned, so did the era of flight. World War I saw the emergence of dogfights and aerial warfare, with pilots engaging in duels in the sky. Synchronized machine gun, a contraption that allowed pilots to shoot through their propellers without turning their aircraft into Swiss cheese. It's not uncommon to magic, except with a lot more bullets.

World War II was a smorgasbord of military innovations. The B-29 Superfortress was like the Rolls-Royce of bombers, boasting remote-controlled turrets and pressurized cabins. And then there's the Jeep, the rugged all-terrain vehicle that could take a beating and keep on rolling. It was the "Jack of all trades" of automobiles, except with more mud.

And there's more! The Cold War brought us a parade of marvels, from the stealthy SR-71 Blackbird, capable of cruising at Mach 3, to the mighty M1 Abrams tank. This hulking juggernaut could take a hit like a linebacker. And who could forget the M16 rifle, the military's attempt at a lightweight, high-capacity firearm that sometimes decided to jam at the worst possible moment?

The Gulf War introduced us to the wonders of GPS technology, making it almost impossible for troops to get lost in the desert – unless they ignored the instructions.

Today, U.S. military innovations continue to amaze and astound, from unmanned drones that can fly missions without a pilot to exoskeletons that turn soldiers into superhumans. But there are some quirky experiments, like the "Gay Bomb" (yes, you read that right), a non-lethal weapon that was supposed to make enemy soldiers irresistibly attracted to each other. It's similar to a plot line from a bad romantic comedy.

U.S. military innovations, a whirlwind journey filled with brilliance, bold experiments, and the occasional bizarre moments. These innovations have shaped the course of history, sometimes with dazzling success and other times with a dash of comedic flair. But one thing's for sure: the quest for military innovation is a never-ending story filled with surprises and questionable moments.

In the crucible of conflict, U.S. military innovations have rewritten the rules of warfare, pushing the boundaries of technology and courage.

War Memorials

Prepare to pay your respects and have your heartstrings tugged as we dive into the history of two iconic U.S. military war memorials – monuments that honor sacrifice and bravery.

First on our tour is the Vietnam Veterans Memorial in Washington, D.C., dedicated in 1982. This somber black wall, designed by Maya Lin, is a minimalist masterpiece that packs a punch. Its sleek design and reflective surface make it seem like a portal to another dimension where you can't help but contemplate the cost of war.

Etched into this eerie, glistening wall are the names of over 58,000 men and women who served and perished in the Vietnam War. A never-ending guest list to the most somber party you'll ever attend. And if you ever find yourself in need of an emotional gut punch, just run your fingers along those names, and you'll be reminded that war is anything but glamorous.

The Vietnam Women's Memorial, a short walk from the wall, honors the more than 265,000 women who served during the war. The statues depict nurses and a wounded soldier, reminding us that war is not just a man's game.

Now, hop over to the West Coast and visit the USS Arizona Memorial in Pearl Harbor, Hawaii. This floating tribute to the heroes of December 7, 1941, is like a history lesson you can walk on. It was dedicated in 1962 and anchored directly above the sunken battleship USS Arizona, which still entombs the remains of over 1,000 servicemen.

Visitors are ferried to the memorial, and it's like stepping onto a hallowed stage. You can peer down into the water and see the ghostly outline of the sunken ship, a chilling reminder of the attack that brought America into World War II. And keep an eye out for the "tears of the Arizona," oil droplets that still seep from the ship's wreckage to this day.

In all seriousness, these memorials serve as important reminders of the sacrifices made by the men and women who served in our nation's wars. They're like open books of history, allowing us to reflect on the past and the price of freedom. So, whether you're standing in silent contemplation before the Vietnam Veterans Memorial or gazing down at the sunken battleship from the USS Arizona Memorial, take a moment to remember the bravery and resilience that make up the story of our military history.

War memorials are the sacred monuments where the sacrifices of heroes are etched in stone, reminding us that freedom comes at a cost.

Disclaimer

This book is intended to entertain, inform, and enlighten readers through the lens of humor and sarcasm. It is not meant to offend, disrespect, or belittle any individuals or professions mentioned within its pages. The goal is to celebrate the dedication, courage, and occasional quirks of first responders, nurses, military personnel, and those in corrections with a lighthearted and playful approach.

Please note that the information presented in this book is accurate to the best of our knowledge at the time of writing. However, the dynamic nature of history and the evolution of these professions may result in changes and updates over time. We recommend consulting authoritative sources for the most current and comprehensive information.

We hope you enjoy this humorous exploration of the past and present, and we extend our gratitude to all those who serve in these vital roles with dedication and valor.

Anthony Bashford

Made in United States
Troutdale, OR
08/21/2024

22207648R00097